KARMIC CAPITALISM

A SPIRITUAL APPROACH TO FINANCIAL INDEPENDENCE

Dr. Bruce Goldberg

Published by

Bruce Goldberg, Inc.
4300 Natoma Ave.
Woodland Hills, CA 91364
Telephone: (800) KARMA-4-U or
FAX: (818) 704-9189
Email: drbg@sbcglobal.net
Web Site:
www.drbrucegoldberg.com

Printed in the United States of America

ISBN 1-57968-122-0

Note to Reader:

This book is the result of the professional experiences accumulated by the author since 1974, working individually with over 14,000 patients. The material included here is intended to complement, not replace, the advice of your own physician, psychotherapist, or other health care professional, whom you should always consult about your circumstances prior to starting or stopping any medication or any other course of treatment, exercise regimen, or diet.

At times, the masculine pronoun has been used as a convention. It is intended to imply both male and female genders where this is applicable.

Some of the minor details in the case histories have been altered to protect the privacy of the author's patients. All of the names used, except those of the celebrities mentioned, have been altered. Everything else in these pages is true.

CONTENTS

INTRODUCTION

This book presents paradigms and techniques to attract abundance and grow spiritually. One thing you will quickly observe as you incorporate these concepts is that your life will change.

I present cutting edge New Age methods to instruct you how to get what you want from life materialistically, while working within the laws of the universe. You will be trained to use your subconscious and Higher Self to globally assess any situation, decide on a game plan for success and take immediate action to convert these lessons into material success.

Less than one percent of Americans possess and control half of its wealth. This book teaches you how to gain a greater sense of your soul's purpose with more drive, focus and success than you have ever experienced. You will be taught how to access your Higher Self and consistently think in new ways, as well as how to capitalize financially on these insights by initiating new actions.

Throughout this book I will explain and illustrate the universal principles that govern financial abundance and spiritual growth. The profile of extremely wealthy people will be used to drive these points home. Many cases drawn from my own therapy practice will further demonstrate how you can apply these easy-to-use methods for yourself.

If you are interested in eliminating "self-defeating sequences" that have acted as obstacles to your success and fulfillment, then read on. If you would like to increase your motivation, make more money in less time, reduce financial and other stresses, obtain any job you desire, attract higher quality people into your life, create abundance and become enlightened spiritually, then this book is for you.

By becoming psychic empowered, you will learn to take charge of your life and experience a future of adventure and challenge, rather than one of maintenance and boredom. You, and not the world around you, will establish goals and make them happen. Previous victimization and other dysfunctional patterns will be removed from your awareness.

The principles described throughout this book have several sources. On the clinical level, I draw from the more than 11,000 individual patients I have had the pleasure to work with since 1974. Theoretical paradigms linking spirituality to abundance emanate from the following sources:

Plato
I Ching or the Book of Changes
Upanishads
The Bhagavad Gita
Corpus Hermeticum
Confucius

You might be wondering if you should read this book. Although the principles presented cover a wide range of business applications, the following groups of people and organizations will benefit from the information herein presented:

- Employees
- Business School Professors
- MBA Students
- CEOs
- Corporate Executives
- Entrepreneurs
- Small Business Owners
- Consultants
- Clergy
- Writers, Media, Press
- Government Agencies
- Organizations
- Any individual who seeks fulfillment in life

Read on and introduce yourself to a world beyond your wildest dreams. See the light at the end of the tunnel and master life changing methods that benefit both you and the universe. Here are just some of the methods you will acquire by practicing the many exercises presented in this book:

- Learn how to be more creative and productive.
- Discover how to bring spirituality into the workplace to effect win-win-win situations.
- Experience both professional and personal rejuvenation.
- Become more empowered and successful, and generate these effects to others.
- Regain control over your soul's direction and purpose.

• Learn techniques to manage difficult people and circumstances to a mutually beneficial resolution.

• Learn techniques of self-hypnosis to program your subconscious mind to make dynamic changes in your being and attract abundance.

• See how small and large corporations utilize karmic capitalism to thrive and become industry leaders, while simultaneously empowering their employees.

This book is about integration. It brings you back to the basics of establishing spirituality and a life purpose, characterized by values and ethics. From this foundation empowerment and abundance techniques are taught. Your relationship with money is reflected in the sense of satisfaction and fulfillment that you get from your connection to your family, your community and the planet. It is based on the energy you send out to the universe, and that is where spiritual growth enters the equation.

Once you have raised the level of your soul's growth through following the simple steps presented in this book, your relationship with money and the universe will change, both for the better. You are about to enter a new level of competence, comfort and consciousness concerning money and spiritual evolvement. Be prepared for the experience of a lifetime.

CHAPTER 1

WHAT IS KARMIC CAPITALISM?

Most people spend at least half their waking hours working at their chosen vocation. The combination of moral stress and less security in the workplace has deleteriously affected productivity and facilitated burnout. It is well established that in order to be more productive, we must love what we do.

Incorporating spirituality in the workplace has not been common, because of preconceptions of a cosmological set of beliefs and inabilities to see how this would improve worker production. Today things are rapidly changing.

Corporations all over the world are making profound changes in order to foster inspiration, productivity, meaning and connection, because they recognize that the old "command and control" models no longer work. More and more people are starting to realize that fostering spirit in the workplace leads to increased happiness and creativity and subsequent increased productivity and profitability.

Comprised spirituality is exhibited in the workplace as high absenteeism, power struggles, low productivity, low morale, gossiping and high turnover rates. Some examples of spiritual principles being applied to professional pursuits include honesty, respect, openness, compassion, commitment to quality and equality, commitment to the environment, and high codes of ethics.

The real question to ask is not "Does spirituality belong in the workplace?" but "Can business thrive without spiritual growth?"

We can look to the Chinese I Ching as a source of using spirituality to empower ourselves. This brilliantly written ancient book of philosophy taught how to look into our own heart to overcome any fear of circumstances that originate outside ourselves.

The key to abundance is represented by this principle from antiquity. It is no wonder that both Confucius and Lao Tzu referred to this book in seeking their own counsel. Western business paradigms consider this as representing the very antithesis of methods for achieving success.

Direct practical business applications are what we will now deal with in presenting principles of karmic capitalism. We can define karmic capitalism as a form of abundance and financial independence obtained as a result of spiritual growth. By spiritual growth I am referring to a raising of the quality of our soul's energy——a purification of sorts.

Many of you reading this book are intelligent enough, educated enough, well experienced in your field and possibly very self-confident about your professional talents. The problem is that whatever you are doing is not satisfying your psyche spiritually or existentially. To obtain this universal form of competitive edge, you are going to have to do something different.

Life-driven business philosophies incorporating spirituality will be, in my opinion, the most sought-after perk of the twenty-first century. As CEOs realize that a positive correlation exists between spiritual growth and net profits, they will welcome this approach. If they do not, their competitors will.

Karmic capitalism always results in an increase in creativity and personal satisfaction from business pursuits. This also corresponds with better morale, lower accident rates, less absenteeism, etc.

Fear-driven behaviors have always dominated the business world. Just consider the stock market fluctuations due to rumors and political events, as an example. Many workers become addicted to these comfortable, yet dysfunctional, modes of behavior. The status may be easy to live with, but it is rarely satisfying.

You may find your actions characterized by saying no to yourself, as well as to others in the workplace. This form of self-abandonment is a type of victimization that leads to depression and other neurotic expressions.

A form of empowerment is needed here to rejuvenate you and get you back on track. It is only when you are willing to face your fears that these new levels of empowerment surface.

An excellent example of this principle was exhibited by one of my patients, named Sara. She was deathly afraid of spiders. During a business meeting she was presented with an assignment to sign to consolidate a deal that had already been approved.

Her lawyer had recommended she sign the contract, but Sara just couldn't bring herself to do it. During a break she went to the coffee machine to refill her cup when suddenly a tarantula walked right by her right leg.

Sara panicked and had to lie down for a while. The people hosting this meeting apologized for this incident, and remarked that in the five years they had been in this office, this was the first time a tarantula had been spotted.

This incident stimulated Sara to reevaluate her fears. She calmed down and eventually signed the contract. To this day her fear of spiders has ceased. All of this occurred prior to my working with her!

For those of you that question the incorporation of spirituality in business, consider the transcendental philosophy of Freemasonry. The origins of our economic system can be traced back to Freemasonry, and its connection between spiritual concepts and economic success.

Freemasonry was a critical component of the American democratic experiment initiated by its founding fathers. This philosophic base takes its roots from the Egyptian mystery religions of antiquity. The Freemasonry of the eighteenth century was both esoteric and political, contrary to the social emphasis of contemporary Masonic lodges.

The main theme of Freemasonry was that there are transcendental realms of reality in which we coexist. We have the potential of tapping into these dimensions to access the wisdom of the universe. It is through our Higher Self (the perfect component of our soul's energy) that we can attain this universal knowledge. This knowledge, in turn, assists us in directing events in our world and is a perfect source of guidance.

Freemasonry was widespread throughout Europe 200 years ago, and focused on the development of human knowledge, the arts and establishing democratic forms of government. At least 50 of the 56 signers of the Declaration of Independence were Masons. These included George Washington, Benjamin Franklin and all but five of the 55 members of the Constitutional Convention.

The design on the back of the dollar bill accepted in 1935 is one example of the influence of Freemasonry on our government. This great Seal was prepared by the Masons in 1782. In addition to Washington and Franklin and most of the signers of the Declaration of Independence, Freemasons from other countries (Lafayette, for example) supported the American Revolution. This helped to initiate a true democratic government that had not taken root in Europe at that time.

THE GREAT SEAL

The Great Seal shown in Figure 1 offers many examples of symbolism. We see an unfinished pyramid beneath an omnipotent eye of the universe on the back of this bill. The words Novus Ordo Seclorum from Virgil are inscribed here. This translates as "A new order of the ages is born." My analysis of this symbolism represented by the Great Seal of the United States of America is that whatever we accomplish on our own is incomplete unless inspired by our Higher Self or God. The pyramid probably refers to the Great Pyramid of Gizah, personifying the universal wisdom of Hermes.

The words annuit coeptis above this incomplete pyramid is translated as "He [God] looks with favor upon our undertaking." We also see an eagle, but in earlier versions the ancient Phoenix was represented. This symbolism implies a form of enlightenment and attainment of spiritual growth as a natural human aspiration. This new order desires peace, but will defend its integrity from potential enemies, as represented by the olive branch and arrows in the eagle's talons.

We see the words E pluribus unum, "unity from many," symbolizing a nation composed of several states. The spiritual overview and linkage with the Higher Self or God is represented by the 13 original colonies (states) in the form of stars above the eagle's head. This cosmic vision allows a truly democratic government to see the "big picture."

The long black judge's robe and the square hat graduating students wear upon graduation in order to become alumni are also Masonic in origin. Fraternities derive their basis from Freemasonry and its fraternal orders. There are many other examples of Freemasonry in modern society.

VALUES AND KARMIC CAPITALISM

Simply working harder and longer is counterproductive in business. All this leads to is frustration and fatigue, sometimes panic and usually loss of self-control and lowered confidence. By scheduling work slower and more efficiently, concentration is improved and higher morale, greater creativity, fewer errors and accidents are observed.

We simply must have quiet time to create and think. Karmic capitalists decide on an idea and a plan, and do whatever it takes to accomplish this objective. They set down a plan of action and take advantage of every opportunity that will get them to this plan. The true karmic capitalist is persistent, yet retains a high standard of personal values. These values and quality of life considerations do not have to act counter to our ambitions and attainment of abundance. It is from these very qualities that our advancements materialistically will grow.

The challenges faced by workers today are essentially spiritual in nature. Spirituality refers to that deeply alive place within each of us that longs for fulfillment. This inner longing generates a heroic quality that dares us to meet life on life's terms. For many of you this requires a soul searching to locate qualities you did not know you had.

Reaching deep within the recesses of your own heart to venture beyond a status quo lifestyle to reach limits and goals previously unknown to you is not easy for the average worker. You must be willing to venture inward to find these new sources of inspiration. All your fears of change or failure must be conquered.

Fear is the one main enemy of spiritual growth and karmic capitalism. When your business life is driven by your soul's purpose rather than by fear, you have established the win-win-win paradigm I call karmic capitalism. Your new spiritual growth is accompanied by abundance. In fact, the greater the spiritual increase, the more material rewards you will enjoy.

We have been taught in Western society not to trust ourselves——not to trust that we do know what we most deeply desire, and how to resolve our inner conflicts. It has been ingrained within our minds that our fellow men and women possess repressed hostilities and are either dysfunctional or evil. We have also been discouraged from exploring and using our subconscious in business. Rationalization and left brain thinking have always dominated the business community.

Fortunately, today we have access to spiritual principles from ages and cultures that not long ago would have been labeled as "secret knowledge."

These paradigms were used to fight and win wars, to build financial and political dynasties, and to accumulate power, wealth, and to achieve inner peace. In our modern world, business-as-usual just doesn't work anymore.

Commitment can only come from having the deep desire of people to truly work together in a new and different way. This groundwork has been laid by philosophers, spiritual leaders, psychologists, activists, visionaries, and futurists, who have led the way by proposing that we humans are eager to demonstrate our basic goodness. We are connected to one another in ways that expand the concept of community to include the entire universe.

Our own inner wisdom originating from our Higher Self directs us to act on universal truths greater than ourselves. These ultimate truths allow for our full potential as a soul to be realized. This results in the karmic capitalist initiating courageous actions on behalf of himself or herself and for others.

Now we can comprehend the fact it is not technology that will conquer the universe, but our ability to access our own Higher Self. The new physics teaches us that we create our own reality. This is the arena of spirituality.

When you practice spirituality principles the universe will always reward your efforts. In December of 1986 I tried to buy a foreclosure property before the auction, but the couple who owned this house would not sell. This foreclosure auction was eventually postponed by their declaring bankruptcy.

Three months later the auction was rescheduled and this same couple called my office late one evening in panic. I informed them that I would clear their liens and save them the embarrassment of the auction and subsequent eviction if they signed the deed over to me. As this house required considerable repairs, I offered no additional funds for their equity.

My further consideration was that I would allow them to rent the house back from me at a lower than market rent. They agreed and I stopped the auction and immediately cleared the liens and took title to the house.

They lived in that house for a year before finally moving back to the midwest. It seemed that a better job opportunity came "out of nowhere" to give this couple a chance to move on with their lives. I had my contractor fix up the house (at a time when he was in need of money to pay off his wife's medical bills) and quickly sold this property with a handsome profit. My additional karmic reward came in the form of a gourmet dinner prepared by the contractor's wife, and a booking on a nationally televised talk show that I had been trying to get on for over a year!

We now have the mechanism to extract from within our very being the way to complete fulfillment——karmic bliss. The karmic capitalist is beginning to make his and her mark on the business world. Each and every one of these spiritual entrepreneurs learn how to tap inner resources that allow them to make better business decisions, to find the most creative solutions, and to inspire those with whom they work.

Our greatest business success will materialize when we remove the previous dysfunctional beliefs and replace them with spiritual ones. Throughout this book I will present examples and techniques to accomplish this goal. There need be no discrepancy between spirituality and success in the workplace.

Real leadership from a karmic capitalistic perspective arises by empowered individuals rising to his or her own highest level of development, and inspiring others to do the same. We have inherited from postmedieval Western civilization a contemporary work ethic built upon the old-paradigm premise that if you work hard and smart enough, you can control the things that happen to you, thus eliminating pain and discomfort. The problem arises when something goes wrong, as it inevitably will. Now fear replaces the desire to perform. It is only when we eliminate the energy drain from this self-perpetuating anxiety and tap into our inner wisdom that our true potential becomes available to us.

If you can retain your belief that this is a loving universe and that the obstacles you face, while apparently steering you in a direction other than where it is you wish to go, are part of a bigger picture than you can yet understand what spirituality entails. For example, when your business is slow, instead of whining or worrying about this downturn, use this time for future planning, preparation and creative brainstorming. Practice the Scout creed of "Be prepared." When things pick up, and they inevitably will, then you will be ready for the increased activity without the additional stress.

If you believe that this is a universe that rewards and punishes, based on your "good" or "bad" behavior, you will be trapped in the old paradigm. This simply does not work; it never did. Fear dominates this mentality, and I have previously pointed out that fear is our only real enemy.

The karmic capitalist has faith and is willing to adopt new beliefs. One belief that now becomes a part of this mind set is that the universe does not offer conditional rewards for good behavior. It supports us unconditionally day in and day out.

Try adopting this belief and acting as if it were an absolute fact. By assuming the universe wants you to succeed, you will find yourself more willing to take risks and convert your ideas into reality. In addition, your inner wisdom will instruct you on how to set limits and to protect yourself from those less evolved souls that attempt to abuse or manipulate you.

I discussed before how working too long and hard was counterproductive. Much of our daily itinerary is no more than busy work. This exhausts us and interferes with our spiritual and creative paths. There is a form of what we in hypnosis refer to as the Law of Reversed Effect: The harder we try to do something, the more elusive the goal becomes.

You must cease and desist those attempts to try to use your good behavior to assure your fate. It is neither necessary nor desirable to attempt to control the outcome of everything in your business life. As we say in Los Angeles, "Work with me."

A regaining of your clarity will result from this becoming part of the universe's flow of energy. You will begin to see not only your faults and weaknesses but also the truth about your strengths and the ways you can contribute to the greater good as well. This is the key to fueling your ambition with inspiration rather than fear.

Just think about how many of the long hours that you invest in your business are fueled by inspiration——how many by fear? Fear can manifest itself in being dishonest with others, as well as yourself. For example, if you are working for someone else, do not be afraid to let your employer or supervisor know that you are having difficulty. This helps that person have a realistic expectation of when the job might be finished. If you give an expectation that is not realistic, then disappointment follows the deception. Being honest toward yourself, and to others, is the most loving thing you can do. It is a basic skill that we should all learn.

Always remember that fear is the memory of past pain, or failure projected into the future. The belief that being honest will result in some form of punishment is a false belief. If your being honest and outspoken resulted in your being fired, you are better off without this position.

When our fear beliefs prevent us from saying what we feel, we block the outward flow of thought energy and store it in our emotions (an emotion is an unexpressed thought). We feel frustrated and angry (a feeling of not being cared for) but are afraid to release our unexpressed thoughts because of the imagined consequences. As a result, we keep quiet and adapt to living in fear. Our mind becomes a pressure cooker of unexpressed thoughts and our blood pressure rises. We believe that there is nothing we can do about the situation.

Fear always works against us. Unless you are facing a physically dangerous situation, fear simply represents insecurity. Many people respond to their own fears by displacing anger onto others. When you love yourself and access your Higher Self daily you give yourself permission to freely express your thoughts and take care of your own needs. This removes any tendency to project negative energy onto subordinates, or anyone else with whom you come into contact.

Karmic capitalism encompasses a wide range of spirituality, which improves our self-image. Our thoughts create our reality. A high level of self-esteem attracts positive and loving situations. Fearful and negative thoughts have the opposite effect.

We can look to Nathaniel Branden's thesis in his The Six Pillars of Self Esteem for specific strategies to raise our self-image. He talks about the following approaches to achieve this goal:

1.   Self-responsibility. By self-responsibility we affirm the fact that we are our own reality. It is our own actions that determine the level of fulfillment we experience.

2.   Personal integrity. Integrity is defined as a compatibility between our thoughts, words, actions and beliefs. This is the opposite of hypocrisy. Pain and suffering is to be expected when this principle is violated. We cannot achieve spiritual growth without a high level of personal integrity.

3.   Self-assertiveness. When we treat ourselves with respect by giving ourselves the right to say no, we eliminate the tendency to be victimized and facilitate a more beneficial participation in the universe.

4.   Living consciously. When we accept the fact that our beliefs are based on the subjective interpretation of our experiences and our emotions simply reflect these beliefs, we are living consciously. These beliefs may or may not accurately represent reality.

5.   Living purposefully. To live purposefully is to consciously decide what our purpose in life is. I use the term karmic purpose to describe the true reason why our soul chose this lifetime to manifest our spiritual growth.

6.   Self-acceptance. The energy we project onto the world we come into contact with will reflect back on us in our experiences. Denying those parts of our consciousness that we do not like manifests itself by its very expression in others that we meet in life. "What goes around comes around."

These six factors are all components of our self-image. If you look upon yourself as not capable of attaining business success, your reality as well will reflect this low self-worth. Your world will be characterized by repeated failures and frustration. It is only when you raise your level of spirituality and learn to love yourself that this cycle ends and abundance becomes your reality.

There are many people who attain abundance, but are personally miserable. My Los Angeles practice daily receives calls from very materialistically successful actors, sports figures, politicians, CEOs and other celebrities. No matter how much fame and fortune they receive, there is never enough to prevent them from sabotaging their life and experiencing depression. A reading of your local newspaper or watching the television news will confirm this fact.

It is not easy for individuals who are unhappy to perceive themselves as desirable and empowered. All previous limiting and self-defeating beliefs must be abandoned and replaced with positive beliefs for a permanent spiritual growth and change to occur. This can easily be accomplished through contacting your Higher Self.

You must accept the fact that to grow spiritually, change is in order. None of us is perfect. We can all learn and improve the quality of our soul's growth. As a therapist I deal with this issue daily. My role is to train my patients to access their Higher Self with a simple technique I refer to as the superconscious mind tap or "cleansing." This script is presented in chapter 2.

One advantage of communicating with your Higher Self is that it facilitates an aligning of your personality with your soul's karmic purpose. This fulfills Branden's living purposefully concept and encourages your spiritual unfoldment. The only true enemy you face in this evolution process is your collective defense mechanisms or ego. This conscious mind proper, as I call it, will do everything in its power to fight change. It responds out of fear and insecurity. By practicing the superconscious mind tap technique you are effectively overpowering this ego and allowing your Higher Self to raise the quality of the soul's energy. This is cleansing and spiritual growth. Once your soul's energy is raised, it cannot be lowered. It may stay at this new level ("plateauing"), or it can be raised to a higher level ("major breakthrough").

Karmic capitalism cannot be established without incorporating the principle of forgiveness into your life. An unforgiving personality blocks creativity and the attraction of positive opportunities into your life. It promotes separation and negativity.

Your ego will naturally try to blame others for circumstances within your own consciousness that created this difficulty in the first place. It is most unfortunate that your ego cannot accept the pain and guilt of its separation from the soul. Guilt is about the misalignment of your personality with your soul. When you blame others and make moral judgments about them, you project onto others the issues you are dealing with in your own life. The world in which we all live is merely a reflection of the energy represented by our soul. To find the origins of a problem, look within your own soul, which acts as a "mirror of karma."

The best way to deal with a problem in a business situation is to first admit to the other party that a problem exists. Next, provide a nonthreatening and nonjudgmental summary of this challenge. For emphasis, you may add how this issue makes you feel.

Communication is critical to success in any aspect of life. Request feedback from your associate, and listen carefully to your assessments. Since you need to reach an understanding of each other's perspective as well as compromise, recognize the fact that each of your views represents the reality you both created. Neither view may be the truth.

This approach establishes an open dialogue and creates avenues toward the possibility of a successful resolution to the problem. If the other person shows no interest in making your mutual relationship better, leave this situation without expressing or harboring any form of negative energy. It is important to recognize the fact that this soul may not want to grow. Always try to raise that person's level up to yours. Never lower your ethics or standards just to satisfy the lack of spirituality of others. If you do, you will find this to be a bottomless pit that can only lead to unhappiness.

Your forgiveness must be unconditional to qualify as karmic capitalism. The other party in my example could not work with you because the fears were too great. Understand that person, do not hate him or her for the lack of spiritual unfoldment. You, in effect, release any pain with your being by unconditionally forgiving that person. This act of self-love will result in your feeling better and becoming more connected with your Higher Self and the universe.

Spirituality teaches us that our thoughts in the form of beliefs create our reality and determine the type of energy we send out to the universe. We have the innate potential to create a positive reality by altering our beliefs. We will deal with specific techniques to bring this about in chapter 5. By effectively reprogramming our subconscious, we can all select a different way of responding to life's challenges. We may then bring about abundance and other changes and become a karmic capitalist.

THE BANKER WITH A HEART

A banker named Ben from the East Coast contacted my office to work on stress reduction and depression. He was a loan officer for a small bank and lost his love of life. His position did allow him some discretion concerning the loan applications he reviewed, but he always seemed to take a hard line approach and quickly rejected any borderline situation.

We worked on several issues, and I described the concept of karmic capitalism to him. Ben was open to this idea and promised me he would lighten up his attitude upon his return home. It took several years before I heard from him.

Ben called me late one evening to inform me of a very desirable promotion he received with a new career. He now worked as a mortgage broker and tripled his income. The reason he obtained this position can be traced back to karmic capitalism.

Shortly after our working together, Ben approved a borderline loan to a young entrepreneur for real estate investments. The old Ben would have rejected this application, but Ben's Higher Self strongly advised he approve it.

The deal was successful and the young entrepreneur named Vic bankrolled his profits into larger and larger deals with each successful loan. Over a period of about four years Vic became a millionaire and never forgot Ben's kindness. Vic always used Ben for his loans and eventually arranged for Ben to land the lucrative mortgage broker position. None of this would have occurred if not for Ben's application of the basic principles of karmic capitalism. "What goes around comes around."

Up to this point we have been focusing on the spiritual component of karmic capitalism. Let us now turn to the abundance part of this paradigm.

Ninety-five percent of the money in the world is controlled by 5 percent of its population. About 50 percent of the world's financial assets are controlled by a mere 1 percent of its people. If there is a dominating factor in being wealthy, it's communication. Since most of your abundance will be derived from others, effective communication is one key to financial independence.

One component of effective communication is the ability to inspire others to be the very best at their chosen field, and to convince them that your business proposal fits within their interests. In professional athletics the coaches and managers that illustrate this principle end up with championships.

Your ability to communicate or to persuade yourself to take specific actions, and your ability to communicate and to persuade others to take a specific action are a direct result of the energy you send out. We have previously discussed this concept. It should, therefore, not be surprising to

21

learn that some of the highest paid and most powerful people in America are communicators and public speakers. One of the reasons for this relates to the tendency of people to pay money to see and hear others doing things that frighten them. The most common fear exhibited by most of us is the fear of public speaking, of getting up in front of a group of strangers and embarrassing ourselves. This also explains why entertainers and professional athletes are so well paid.

Capitalism is built upon the ability to transform ideas into a product or service that fulfills a demand. Economists call this the law of supply and demand. When we add spirituality to this equation, the term karmic capitalism becomes relevant.

The likelihood of your becoming successful in some entrepreneurial pursuit, or in moving up the corporate ladder, depends upon your ability to develop beliefs that both perceive this goal and affirm your ability to attain it.

It is next to impossible to create substantial wealth from your labors alone. There just aren't enough hours in the day. Throughout this book I will reinforce the principle that overworking yourself is never the answer to success. It only breeds dysfunctional behavior.

Altering your thoughts to an abundance mindset is far more efficient and healthy in producing wealth. When I submitted the manuscript for my first book, Past Lives——Future Lives, back in 1981, I received 48 rejections! My belief in its efficacy and marketability never wavered. Two acceptances did eventually arrive. To this date that book has earned me over two million dollars! The main point I am trying to make here is to practice what you preach, utilize your Higher Self, be persistent and apply spirituality to all aspects of your life.

Even with all of those four dozen rejections, I continued to be positive and act as if my book had been accepted. I write all of my books and conduct all interviews with the media from the perspective of my Higher Self. That technique will be presented in several different ways throughout this book, especially chapter 5.

Karmic capitalism requires you to be an empowered soul. Being empowered also involves acting in a decisive manner. Those businessmen and women that I judge to be successful always make decisions quickly. They also waste very little time in their decision-making process.

Unless you are a true visionary, when you get an idea it has already been put into the universe. That means several others are sharing the same idea. The person who capitalized on the idea first is the one who achieves the greatest amount of financial reward. It is not uncommon in business and research to discover several different people working independently on the same idea. These individuals are not in direct contact with each other, in fact, they are competitors.

One must keep an open mind must be kept to truly capitalize on decision making. You can never advance your position by saying no. It is only with an affirmative response that you can move forward. Saying no only maintains your current position. If there is no downside (potential for loss of money, resources or time), then your answer should always be yes.

Fear prevents less empowered souls from being decisive. They're afraid they'll make the wrong decision, and that very fear will lead them to think that any decision they make will have been the wrong one. Since they are programmed negatively with very limited beliefs, they eventually end up with the consequences they fear the most. It's that "mirror of karma" principle in action.

Even mistakes resulting from quick decisions can be educational. Karmic capitalists learn to make a further decision to correct their previous error, or minimize the loss, and can still grow by taking with them the knowledge they obtained from the previous decision.

Life, including business, is a numbers game. You can't win them all, and you don't have to in order to attain wealth. Making decisions quickly will always put you in a place to win as opposed to your making no decisions at all. This personality style, interestingly enough, prevents burnout.

Another way to prevent job burnout is to love what you do. Even if you are required to work long hours, your day will go faster and you will be less fatigued. Part of karmic capitalism is to move toward achieving your soul's purpose (karmic purpose). Karmic capitalists would always choose to do what they are now doing, if given a choice to begin their career all over again. Always remember that life is about experiences, and the more experiences you have reaching your goals, the more you'll understand what you want and don't want in life.

Another characteristic of karmic capitalists is their continued striving to be the very best in their field. By doing more than you're paid for, you are effectively building up your self-confidence and simultaneously improving your skills.

Even if you dislike your current position, this overdelivering and underpromise approach will assist you in being promoted to a higher level, or presented with a better job offer by a competitor. Spirituality principles continually demonstrate that if you do more than you're being paid for, you'll get what you deserve. What goes around comes around.

In order to effectively influence others and attain abundance, there are certain principles that must be followed to be in alignment with karmic capitalism. Here are some of these paradigms:

1.   Always know your bottom line. Have a specific point at which you are not willing to give up any more than this value to obtain your goal. Draw your karmic "line in the sand."

2.   Have a good idea of other people's desires. Try to match your goals with theirs. Whenever you can, give the people what they want.

3.   Prepare a specific goal to be attained. If the other party knows better than you what you want, your actions are automatically compromised.

4.   Look upon any setback as feedback. This is an important belief. Learn from all your past mistakes and stay positive. The late Vince Lombardi never lost a football game. Occasionally, he "ran out of time."

5.   Always be professional. Never allow emotions to interfere with a business decision or relationship. Becoming overexcited or angry in any situation clouds your judgment and diminishes your influence.

6.   Take responsibility for all of your actions. Nobody likes or respects someone blaming others. Karmic capitalists admit their errors and never shift the blame. The last thing any business executive wants to hear is "My dog ate my homework."

7.   Be open to alternate plans to accomplish your goal. The best-laid plans of mice and men often go astray. Be prepared with plan B, plan C and so on in case your original approach proves useless.

8.   Never manipulate others. If you attempt to use others, you will never be a karmic capitalist. All business deals should have a win-win motive. It is fine to let the other party think your plan was his or her idea. However, if this offer cannot pass the "Would I want to be persuaded to take the action or hold the belief that I'm asking others to hold?" test, then withdraw this proposal or alter it so it does meet this criteria.

Karmic capitalists are always promoting themselves and what they are doing. Since they are proud of what they do, they let other people know what they're going for. By putting it out you open the doors of opportunity for others to share your passion and give support to your goals. Enlist the aid of all who are in a position to help you. For example, when I am interviewed on the radio, I give out my toll-free telephone number, which is 1-800-KARMA 4 U. The host usually laughs and repeats the number several times commenting on how creative and symbolic it is of my work. The audience now has ample opportunity to write it down. Karmic capitalism has many interesting facets.

CHARACTERISTICS OF EMPOWERED PEOPLE

To be a karmic capitalist, you must become empowered. Here are some characteristics of individuals who have mastered the art of empowerment. See how many of these traits you possess currently:
- They never procrastinate.
- They do not waste their time wishing that they hadn't done something.
- They are doers, and are almost always engaged in work that will make other people's lives more pleasant or the universe a better place to live.
- They can admit to making mistakes.
- They are free from guilt and worry.
- Any potential setback or problem is viewed as an obstacle to be overcome.
- Business plans are constructed on a win-win-win basis.
- They function on high energy, and are truly excited about everything they do.
- They do not need to be loved by everyone.
- They are not afraid to fail.
- They do not blame others, they help others and themselves to assign responsibility where it belongs.
- They are creative and encourage spiritual growth in others.
- They are open to change and new paradigms.
- They are never satisfied with the status quo.
- They are healthy and always look younger than their chronological age.
- They are karmic capitalists with spiritual lifestyles that are never compromised for the purpose of attaining wealth.

Ken Blanchard contributed an excellent example of karmic capitalism to Chicken Soup for the Soul at Work. There is a Saturn dealership in Albuquerque, New Mexico, that prides itself on its 72 percent of first-time visitors returning for a second visit. This far exceeded the 8 percent rate for all dealerships in town.

This unique dealership was also posting sales of six to eight new cars daily six days a week in a slumping car market. Saturn did not achieve this feat simply by being easy to negotiate with, since they featured a "no-dicker sticker" policy. There was no possibility of lowering the price placed on the car window. Furthermore, their salespeople were salaried, so commission mentality was removed as a motivating factor.

One Milt Garrett decided one Sunday to purchase a new car for his wife to celebrate her fifth anniversary of being cancer free. He informed the dealership of his plans to surprise his wife, and instructed them not to tell her about it.

The following week he brought his wife, Jane, to the dealership and beamed as she fell in love with a white Saturn coupe. Jane by now expressed interest in purchasing that car. Milt played hard to please, and intimated that they couldn't afford a new car at this time.

When Jane walked around to the front of this car she let out an emotional scream as she read a large engraved sign attached to this car. The sign read:

Congratulations, Jane. This car is yours. Five years cancer free. Let's celebrate life. From Milt, Billy and Team Saturn.

The back of this sign was endorsed by every Saturn employee. In addition, to allow the couple a moment to themselves, the entire store was emptied. Everyone took a break, including the mechanics, clerical staff and receptionist. They all applauded and cried when Jane screamed and gave Milt the biggest hug and kiss he had ever experienced.

This compassion and expression of unconditional love and spiritual growth qualifies as a perfect example of karmic capitalism. Is it any wonder why this dealership does the best business in town?

PROFESSIONAL JEALOUSY

I refer to professional jealousy as the PJ syndrome. It is easier to use these initials when discussing this unfortunate fact of life, so that when you do not want to offend others have no reason to become upset. If they overhear your conversation they will probably assume you are discussing pajamas.

The karmic capitalist need not concern him/herself with the opinion of others. The more you attract abundance and success into your life, the greater will be the frequency of envy exhibited by others who have not matched your success. This is simply a reflection of their insecurities.

Do not be surprised to discover that you no longer share common interests with associates once you achieve the status of a karmic capitalist. The cream has a tendency to rise to the surface. As your soul's energy improves in quality, you will attract kindred colleagues and clients into your life. Look for a decrease in the quantity but an increase in the quality of people in both your professional and personal life as you master the techniques of karmic capitalism.

The superconscious mind tap method functions to align your soul with your Higher Self. This raises the frequency vibrational rate (FVR) of the former, thereby producing a form of spiritual growth. Your new reality is now simply a reflection of your increased awareness to the higher dimensions of consciousness. It is not uncommon for you to experience increased frequency and duration of periods of joy and peace as part of your repowerment.

This method will assist you in dealing with issues such as the PJ syndrome. The universe continually tests us. Do not allow yourself to fall back on emotional responses and second guessing your own karmic purpose. Always hold your head high and move forward along your path to spiritual unfoldment. Attaining abundance is part of your innate right and the universe will cooperate with these goals as long as you practice the ethics and other paradigms of karmic capitalism.

There are certain codes of behavior that need to be adopted if you desire to attain karmic capitalism. This approach is in no way designed to have you gain material possessions at either someone else's or the universe's expense. Here are some principles to live by:

1. Resist the tendency to be ruthless and take advantage of others.

2. Treat others as you would like to be dealt with yourself. "Do unto others...."

3. Go out of your way to assist others.

4. Open your mind to receive guidance from your Higher Self. Practice superconscious mind taps regularly.

5. Practice selflessness and break your own hard-nosed rules once in a while to better the lives of those with whom you come into contact.

6. Always maintain the highest level of integrity in all personal and professional relationships.

7. Eat healthier foods, exercise regularly, think positively and expect the best. For a more detailed discussion of this principle I recommend my book Look Younger, Live Longer.

8. Practice compassion, giving, forgiving, altruism, humility, optimism, noncondemnation and universal love in your daily life.

POSITIONING

Those of you who are familiar with my work with the electronic media know of my many radio and television interviews. An interesting example of karmic capitalism occurred very early in my media career.

Less than two years following my first electronic interview, I booked myself on a local overnight radio talk show. WBAL radio in Baltimore, Maryland, in 1982 was the top-rated talk station. My first interview took place on February 13 at about 12:05 A.M. I stayed on the show until 5:00 A.M. and discussed my work with hypnotic past-life regression and future-life progression.

The host of this show asked me if I would be willing to regress and progress him in exchange for his playing the tapes of these future sessions on the air. I readily agreed. This created quite a bit of interest locally. Little did I know at the time, but the general manager of this conservative station in a nonmetaphysical city personally listened to me on February 13, as well as these taped sessions played on subsequent shows.

His office contacted me and by May of that year I hosted my own five-hour show on WBAL Radio on Saturday nights from midnight to 5:00 A.M. I called my show "Insights into Parapsychology," and conducted live past-life regressions as part of my itinerary. To show you how well the universe received this event, the Associated Press wire service did a feature story on me and my show. This brought national attention to both me and the station. All of this, I feel, was due to the principles of karmic capitalism.

I refer to this concept of being the very best you can be at your chosen craft and letting the universe create an eventual recognition of your work as positioning. If you have a short attention span and demand an immediate fulfillment of your abundance goals, then this approach is not for you. This attitude of "Are we there yet?" is not the demeanor of a karmic capitalist.

Think of a business conversation. If a client, producer, reporter, etc., calls you because he or she wants to do business with or interview you, or perhaps hire you, then your negotiation position is strong. Compare this to your soliciting any of them for some project or interview. Positioning works and represents an important principle of karmic capitalism.

Work with the universe and refrain from acting in a greedy or impatient manner. Maintain all of the qualities of a karmic capitalist and the universe will provide you with abundance and facilitate your spiritual unfoldment.

In the fall of 1994 one of the producers of the NBC daytime talk show The Other Side decided to do a show on progressing into the future. This producer researched the topic and discovered that the first book ever written on taking people into the future of this life, or future lifetimes, was my first book Past Lives-Future Lives.

By writing that book and working within the field for many years, I had positioned myself as the progression authority. The show featured me and three of my patients who had undergone progression hypnotherapy. One woman raised her immune system to fight AIDS, another saved her mother's life by viewing the future and the third patient used this paradigm to find her soul mate.

These cases are detailed in my book Soul Healing. Of importance here are the benefits the network, the universe and I received as a result of the positioning principle. This is an example of a win-win-win concept——karmic capitalism at its best.

THE POINT OF LIGHT TECHNIQUE

Whenever I travel to conduct a workshop I institute a form of karmic capitalism I like to call my "point of light" technique. This entails notifying some people who have contacted my office in reference to my work that I will be in town and would like their assistance during this event.

I select letters from those readers who are unable to attend my speaking engagement because of the cost. This method works well for several reasons.

One obvious implication is that a highly motivated soul now has the opportunity for additional spiritual growth, as all of my various experiential workshops train the attendees to access their Higher Self. I also benefit in having an assistant or two to help with registration and merchandise sales during and following the event.

The assistants have the opportunity to enjoy the workshop throughout, as I only need their service at the beginning, during the break and at the very end of this presentation. Let me illustrate this win-win-win form of karmic capitalism with some specific examples.

In December of 1983 I scheduled an experiential workshop in hypnotic past-life regression and future-life progression to take place in Silver Spring, Maryland (a Washington, D.C., suburb). The month prior to this seminar I received a call from an astrologer who desperately wanted to attend. Her problem was financial.

The universe cooperated in this instance as I had the need for an extra assistant to handle registration and book sales. On November 18 (my birthday) I was interviewed on a local television show (Morning Break), and this resulted in better-than-expected preregistration attendees.

I informed this woman that I would be happy to have her attend this workshop as my guest, if she would agree to function as my assistant. This would allow her to experience the various techniques I presented to the other attendees.

She agreed and was ecstatic. Her personality and efficiency exhibited during this workshop was well received by one and all. This turned out to be one of the most enjoyable workshops I have ever conducted. In addition to it being financially successful (hence its inclusion in this book), the variety of attendees, from wives of ambassadors and politicians to media representatives and others, simply generated tremendous energy and positivity.

Many of these attendees became private patients, and a spiritual growth experience was had by all. An additional reward was presented to me by the universe three and one-half years later. The producer of the Washington, D.C., television show Morning Break went on to New York to work on the Donahue show. She booked me on his show in July 1987. To this day my full hour interview on Donahue, during which I conducted two live past-life regressions, stands out as one of my very best interviews. I say this not only from a financial standpoint, but also in reference to the communication medium and the energy that followed from this exposure.

Those of you who have read my second book, The Search For Grace, are aware that my Donahue interview resulted in sessions with a woman I call Ivy, who came to my office for therapy. Ivy's documented past life was the basis for the CBS movie, Search For Grace, that first aired on the network on May 17, 1994.

Although I have done many live past-life regressions and future-life progressions on radio and television, I have never conducted such a time-travel demonstration without properly preparing the subject beforehand. The universe decided to test my karmic muscle in a most interesting way in 1994.

I was scheduled to conduct an experiential workshop in San Francisco in August of 1994. This was just three months after my CBS movie, Search For Grace, aired. As I described previously when I related my experience in Silver Spring, Maryland, in 1983, I required assistants to help me during this speaking engagement.

Four women who previously contacted my office from San Francisco agreed to assist me in exchange for a free ticket to this event. Three of the four women could not have afforded this relatively inexpensive seminar.

To further promote this event, I booked an interview on San Francisco's highest rated morning radio show, the "Alex Bennett Show." The only catch was that Alex wanted me to regress him live on the air with no prior conditioning. I had never done that before.

During his early morning show on August 8, 1994, I did just that. Alex was somewhat skeptical about the possibility of past-life regression, but nonetheless successfully regressed into the life of a an eighteenth-century composer in Europe. This live and dynamic interview brought several dozen extra attendees into my experiential workshop.

The four assistants at the event did a marvelous job. One of these women, whom I shall refer to as Kay, took charge and directed the other three. Kay was a natural karmic capitalist, and generated quite a few extra sales of books and tapes.

I rewarded each of my helpers with a free copy of my latest book. Kay was given a hypnotic time-travel six-cassette album as a bonus for her executive and marketing skills. Several months later Kay called me to let me know that she had changed jobs for a more enjoyable and lucrative field and offered to remunerate me for the album I gave her.

Naturally, I would not accept her money. I simply thanked her for sharing her success at karmic capitalism. She is one spiritual, bright, personable and quality soul. Her future is a bright and empowering one.

CHAPTER 2

A CRASH COURSE IN METAPHYSICS

Webster's Deluxe Unabridged Dictionary (2nd Edition) defines metaphysics as "the branch of philosophy that deals with the nature of being or reality...." We will apply this ancient discipline to show you how by merely altering your belief systems, a completely different path in life can be created – a path that exhibits karmic capitalism.

Most of the problems we face are due to the attitudes we possess. A limiting belief system will be manifested on our ability to attain any goal, financial or personal. For example, one of my patients firmly believed that because she was a woman, she could not attain a certain executive position with her company. Shortly after successfully programming that limiting belief from her subconscious, she was admitted into an executive training program. We will deal with these benefits in detail in chapter 4.

We must always consider the big picture of how the universe works. The physical, or earth, plane that we live on currently is only one of several dimensions that exist in the ever-expanding universe. I will present techniques to illustrate how a trip to the astral plane during our dream state may effectively affect events on the physical plane. This can be achieved by simply altering our level of consciousness.

Our dreamworld represents a consciousness level in which we can create any scenario we choose. This affords us with an excellent opportunity to use our creativity and facilitate our spiritual growth and abundance. There is a connection between this dreamworld and the physical plane we live on. The subconscious and Higher Self components of our consciousness represent this link.

Because such a linkage between the physical world and dreamworld exists, we can transfer karmic capitalistic traits acquired on the dimension many term the Astral Plane (dreamworld) to our present world. Dreams function as a sneak preview into other realms, and to introduce us to our Higher Self so that we may grow spiritually.

The problem with dreamworld is that it is very responsive to our emotions and imagination. Attaining a higher level of spiritual growth will transform these two factors into allies to facilitate our ability to attract abundance, and still raise our consciousness.

Dreamworld acts as a two-way form of communication. We can program it to assist our training in karmic capitalism. In addition, our subconscious and Higher Self can use the plots played out in this ethereal realm to educate us in our karmic path.

A detailed discussion of this dreamworld, along with dozens of exercises to utilize this nocturnal resting state for growth, is presented in my book Dream Your Problems Away.

To begin using your dreams to attain abundance, consider these simple principles:

• Focus on what you desire to attract abundance in your life prior to retiring.

• Create a sanctuary as a peaceful reference point for your dreams. You can return to this safety zone if the content of
your dream becomes uncomfortable or too cumbersome.

• Use this state to contact your Higher Self.

• Custom design your dreams to fulfill any purpose you like.

• Keep your motives pure and have faith in your ability to create your own reality.

Here is a simple exercise to facilitate your ability to use your dreams for karmic capitalism training:

1. Place your body in the most relaxed state you are capable of by any method that is comfortable for you.

2. In your mind clearly formulate a specific dream that will solve a problem, initiate creativity, or attract abundance into your life.

3. Develop a belief system that removes any doubt about your ability to induce any dream you desire.

4. Edit down your dream theme into a clear, positive and concise phrase. Repeat this phrase several times aloud or to yourself.

5. Focus intensely on this dream theme and visualize your custom designed dream as though it were happening at this very moment. Picture yourself in your mind and feel your body having this dream.

6. Converse with the characters that appear in your dream. Redirect their actions by simply thinking about a subplot to this scenario.

7.   Take over this dream and place your persona in the roles of others in the nightly play, and act in a positive manner to make this a fulfilling experience.

8.   Record your dreams in a journal immediately upon awakening.

9.   During your waking day, engage in activities that reflect the content of your most recent dream. Keep your mind open to any stimulus from your environment that can be used to direct a dream.

The metaphysical theory displayed by dreamworld is one of a different reality than we are used to on the physical plane. Dreamworld illustrates the principle that we are the creator of our events in life. "As above, so below" is the Hermetic expression that describes this concept.

The world that we function on is simply a classroom in the universe's university system. Our purpose is to grow spiritually. To accomplish this goal we must learn many lessons. Successfully learning these cosmic principles, while acting ethically and with a high level of commitment along with creativity and love, will result in financial rewards beyond your wildest expectations.

This system is not designed to make us wealthy, but to train us to become responsible citizens of the universe. By cooperating with the creator of this vast system's paradigm, we achieve a form of psychic empowerment that leads to financial independence, along with spiritual growth and many other benefits.

We can look to Napoleon Hill to illustrate the quantum physics expression that our thoughts create our reality when he stated, "All thoughts which have been emotionalized [given feeling] and mixed with faith, begin immediately to translate themselves into their physical equivalent or counterpart." A more thorough discussion of this concept can be found in my book Soul Healing.

Throughout our life we face events that are the result of our beliefs and powers of imagination. Nothing in the universe occurs as a result of pure chance. Carl Jung would describe these meaningful circumstances without apparent cause as examples of synchronicities.

It is not by accident that our lives are characterized by love, enjoyable professions, good health, plenty of energy and abundance. The reverse also applies. Being victimized by others and failing consistently in business are due to your own actions, fears, negative programming, low self-image and other examples of what I term "self-defeating sequences."

We all experience a certain amount of negative thoughts throughout the day. Do not become anxious about these examples of negative thinking somehow scarring you for life. These fears are not so powerful that they will outweigh the thrust of a basically positive mental climate. Thoughts and emotions have a natural flow. Different types of thoughts and emotions will move and change as long as you do not block them. It's only when you focus on negative thoughts and beliefs that you create difficulties.

Many people are frightened by responsibility. It's far more of a burden to be powerless over the events in your life than to be responsible for them. You have power—power to create changes and make things more to your own design. All you require is the confidence and absence of fear to accomplish this.

To truly comprehend this perfect system of karmic justice and metaphysics, consider the fact that our life's lessons for spiritual growth are presented to us in the classroom we term physical reality. The architect of our experience is thought. It is our thoughts that actually mold and shape the world in which we live. For example, on the astral plane (the dimension we travel to during our dream state, and immediately following physical death) our thoughts immediately materialize into reality.

The problem with our thoughts on the physical plane is that they don't follow this path of immediate materialization, are mostly negative and are based upon our past experiences, most of which are problematic. If this were not true, you wouldn't' be reading this book.

You may point to real examples of how you failed to do something, or an unethical behavior was exhibited by someone you trusted, and use this as a rationalization for your current cynical or negative belief system. Just because this evidence exists does not mean that this belief system is the way things truly are or are meant to be.

In metaphysics we quickly see that belief systems and attitudes can be altered, and when they reflect a positive and empowering paradigm, we are more open to experience joy, fulfillment, creativity and abundance. These are now the truer to the nature of our being.

We are now free to experiment with what works best for us. We are meant to freely play with our ideas, try them, watch them materialize, reevaluate, make changes, and generally focus on a point of view that brings us a fulfilling life. Each and every aspect of our physical reality is changeable by a proper mind set and following the principles and exercises presented in this book.

BASIC METAPHYSICAL BELIEFS

There are three basic metaphysical belief systems that I refer to as Universal Paradigms 1, 2 and 3 or UP-1, UP-2 and UP-3. Here is a brief summary of these beliefs:

UP-1. The basic component of the universe is assumed to be matter-energy. Consciousness arises out of matter (the brain) when man evolved from the lower animals. Matter and energy are interrelated by Einstein's famous equation $E=mc2$, where E=energy, m=matter and c=the speed of light. We refer to this belief as materialistic monism.

UP-2. Dualism is introduced by the matter-energy and mind-spirit components of this paradigm. Modern science investigates matter-energy, but mind-spirit can only be explored through subjective experiences. Thus, two different forms of knowledge surface. Psychic phenomena represent an overlap of these two fields. The Nobel laureate Sir John Eccles was a great advocate of this belief system.

UP-3. Consciousness itself is now assumed to be the main component of the universe. This Universal Mind creates matter-energy, including the physical plane, dreamworld and all of the other realms of the universe. Accessing our Higher Self (a component of the Universal Mind or God) is how we perceive true reality. Consciousness therefore created material evolution! Our five senses are but a part of the illusions of the material world. Transcendental monism is the term used to describe this belief.

Today, Western society is gradually shifting from a UP-1 to a UP-3 belief system. The UP-3 paradigm has never been popular in the West, although it has been presented through the mystery religions, Gnosticism, the Rosicrucians, Freemasonry, New England Transcendentalists of the mid-nineteenth century, Theosophists and Anthroposophy movements of the nineteenth and twentieth centuries.

The question is not so much which of these paradigms are true, but which one best describes the totality of your subjective experience. The reductionist scientific UP-1 and UP-2 approaches fail in this regard. UP-3 is by far more global and compatible to the totality of human experience and spiritual growth.

Today the UP-1 approach is declining, as is the UP-2 belief. We are seeing an upsurge in support for the UP-3 concept. UP-3 is quickly becoming the dominant paradigm not only of this society, but of most of the world as well. It has been around since the dawn of civilization, is a component of most of the world's spiritual traditions and is the basis of karmic capitalism.

In order to create your own reality on an intellectual, emotional and intuitive level, you must trust your inner awareness from your Higher Self and affirm your own being. This tuning into your Higher Self I refer to as a superconscious mind tap. At this level our intellect and intuitive functions merge and we unite with the perfect part of our soul's energy. This is the "divine spark within us." One result of this experience is a "stream of consciousness" that is followed by good fortune and general feelings of optimism, positivity and empowerment.

Throughout this book I will present exercises in accessing your Higher Self to raise the qualities of your soul's energy in order to manifest positive goals, such as abundance. I refer to this as karmic capitalism, since spiritual growth is an ingrained component of this process.

Progressive relaxation is an excellent relaxation technique. It consists of alternately tensing and relaxing various muscles in your body. You can sample this technique by the following exercise:

1.   Tense your toes; hold the tension for a few seconds, then release. Proceed with the entire foot, then calves, thighs, and so on, one part at a time, until you have alternately tensed and then relaxed each portion of your body.

2.   A variation of this technique consists of focusing your mind on each part of your body and deliberately relaxing the muscles there. Continue until you have relaxed each part of your body.

3.   You can also use meditation techniques or rhythmic breathing exercises to get into a relaxed state.

For example, try breathing in deeply, hold your breath for a count of ten and slowly let it out for another count of ten. While you are breathing in this manner perform the progressive relaxation method described in the previous paragraphs.

MEETING YOUR HIGHER SELF

The Higher Self has been called various names. I personally refer to it as the superconscious mind, but it is also known as the God Within, multidimensional self, the divine spark within and several other terms. This perfect part of our soul's energy is our own inner wisdom and spiritual advisor. It communicates to us through the voice of our intuition and our everyday spontaneous inclinations, using the subconscious as its agent.

Since we are only in the beginning stages of understanding the full extent of our beings, our concepts of the larger self are probably only approximations of the real thing. In other words, your Higher Self may not meet you in precisely the terms you prefer; you might not get a formal introduction. Your Higher Self may have its own ideas of how it wants to connect with you.

Here is the script to the superconscious mind tap that I developed in 1977 to train my patients to access their Higher Self:

Now listen very carefully. I want you to imagine a bright white light coming down from above and entering the top of your head. Filling your entire body. See it, feel it and it becomes reality. Now only your masters and guides and highly evolved loving entities who mean you well will be able to influence you during this or any other hypnotic session. You are totally protected by this aura of pure white light.

In a few moments I am going to count from 1 to 20. As I do so you will feel yourself rising up to the superconscious mind level where you will be able to receive information from your Masters and Guides. You will also be able to overview all of your past, present and future lives. Number 1 rising up. 2, 3, 4 rising higher. 5, 6, 7, letting information flow. 8, 9, 10, you are half way there. 11, 12, 13, feeling yourself rising even higher. 14, 15, 16, almost there. 17, 18, 19 number 20 you are there. Take a moment and orient yourself to the superconscious mind level.

PLAY NEW AGE MUSIC FOR 1 MINUTE

You may now ask yourself any question about any past, present or future life issue. Or, you may contact any of your guides or departed loved ones from this level. You may explore your relationship with any person. Remember, your superconscious mind level is all knowledgeable and has access to your akashic records.

Now slowly and carefully state your desire for information or an experience and let this superconscious mind level work for you.

PLAY NEW AGE MUSIC FOR 8 MINUTES

You have done very well. Now I want you to further open up the channels of communication by removing any obstacles and allowing yourself to receive information and experiences that will directly apply to and help better your present lifetime. Allow yourself to receive more advanced and more specific information from your Higher Self and Masters and Guides to raise your frequency and improve your karmic subcycle. Do this now.

PLAY NEW AGE MUSIC FOR 8 MINUTES

Alright now. Sleep now and rest. You did very very well. Listen very carefully. I'm going to count forwards now from 1-5. When I reach the count of 5 you will be back in the present, you will be able to remember everything you experienced and re-experienced you'll feel very relaxed refreshed, you'll be able to do whatever you have to planned for the rest of the day or evening. You'll feel very positive about what you've just experienced and very motivated about your confidence and ability to play this tape again to experience the superconscious mind level. Alright now. 1 very very deep, 2 you're getting a little bit lighter, 3 you're getting much much lighter, 4 very very light, 5 awaken. Wide awake and refreshed.

KARMIC CAPITALISM RESULTING FROM PSYCHIC ABILITIES

Spirituality and consciousness research has revealed that science is compatible with the distilled experience of many inner explorers over thousands of years. None of the traditional UP-1 scientific models adequately depict all aspects of reality. The new physics (quantum physics) has demonstrated that if two particles have been intimately associated and are then separated in space, they are "connected" nonetheless. Destroying an electron by observing it results in the annihilation of a positron, without subjecting the latter to the destructive process of the electron microscope. A positron is identical to an electron, except that the former spins in the opposite direction as the electron and has the opposite charge.

In addition to further establishing the interconnectedness of these two subatomic particles, Feynmann hypothesized that this established the fact that positron was merely the electron moving backward in time and vice versa. This connectedness also gave rise to the possibility that the electron was traveling faster than the speed of light (something Einstein considered impossible) and this resulted in reverse time sequences. I use this paradigm to explain how my patients can view their own future through hypnosis – something I call progression hypnotherapy.

Bell's theorem in quantum physics states that everything in the universe is connected. It denounces the "principle of local causes", which holds that a phenomenon can be explained in terms of causes in the immediate space-time location. For example, the results of an experiment conducted in one location would not be expected to be affected by what is happening at some spot in the universe remote in space or time or both. The physicist David Bohm states that particles and energy fields by themselves are inadequate in explaining reality. A non-reductionist "unbroken wholeness" paradigm must be included in our depiction of reality.

In developing our innate abilities of karmic capitalism, we must tap into our paranormal capacities. These exceptional talents allow us to do things we find fantastic and nearly unbelievable when evaluated by our rational mind. These capacities include creative functions, intuition, altruistic spirit and unusual mastery of mind-body functions.

Much research has been done to explore this paradigm and the precise nature of these exceptional abilities. The results of these experiments have already resulted in far-reaching implications for science, education, sports, individual health and well-being and business.

The principles of karmic capitalism probably are difficult for the uninitiated and conventionally trained business person to accept. Since they are affected to a certain degree by psychic phenomena, here is a classification of psychic abilities:

1.   Channeling or mediumship. This is a communication with discarnate entities, occasionally accompanied by physical or quasi-physical phenomena.

2.   Extrasensory perception (ESP). Data is obtained by something other than our five senses:

A. Retrocognition. Memories of past events are obtained through some unknown source. I refer to this as regression.

B. Precognition. Images of future events are accurately depicted. Progression is the term I use for this phenomenon.

C. Clairvoyance. Information is usually depicted about an event occurring now that is unattainable through the five senses.

D. Clairaudience. Sounds are heard in reference to a current event that are far beyond the range of the ears.

E. Telepathy. Communication is established from one mind to another, so as to accurately read another's thoughts.

3.   Psychokinesis. A physical effect on an object established solely through efforts of the mind:

A. Basic psychokinesis . Metal bending, compass movements and other movements of objects with no physical contact.

B. Levitation. Elevating one's body off the ground.

C. Materialization and dematerialization. The appearance and disappearance of an object by thought projection.

D. Teleportation. A disappearance of an object from one specific location and its subsequent reappearance at another spot.

E. Thought photography. Using mental projection of thoughts to impart an image on photographic film.

F. Psychic healing. This includes laying on of hands, absent healing and many other such types as I described in my book Soul Healing.

The categories marked with an asterisk (*) are commonly utilized in karmic capitalism, and will be presented throughout this book. Although conventional UP-1 science has never demonstrated these phenomena to their satisfaction, all of these have been reported by a variety of civilizations over thousands of years. We must bear in mind that quantum physics teaches us that the mind of the observer affects the outcome of an observation!

We can turn to the respected parapsychological researcher H. J. Eysenck, head of the Department of Psychology at Maudsley hospital in London. When he averred: "Unless there is a gigantic conspiracy involving 30 university departments all over the world, and several hundred highly respected scientists in various fields, many of them originally hostile to the claims of the psychic researchers, the only conclusion the unbiased observer can come to must be that there are people who obtain knowledge existing in other people's minds, or in the outer world, by means yet unknown to science."

CHANGING BELIEFS

The corporate world can sometimes bring out the worst behavior in people. Janet used her charms and knowledge of human nature to sleep her way up the corporate ladder of success. She very much enjoyed the control she exerted over the men she sexually manipulated.

There was one promotion she desperately desired that just seemed to be out of her reach. That is when she called my office. One of her female colleagues recommended my work to her.

When Janet entered my office, I observed a frustrated and unhappy soul. She even tried to use her charms on me, but to no avail. Interestingly enough, after I confronted her concerning her seduction attempt, she seemed to settle down and become far more open to therapy.

My discussion of karmic capitalism principles were well received by Janet. She knew I had been successful with the colleague who referred her. I trained Janet to access her Higher Self and observed immediate effects of serenity and hopefulness. She was trained to use this superconscious mind connection to formulate a game plan to obtain the position she so desired.

Several months later she called me to let me know that not only did she attain that position, but her attitude and reputation improved. She was no longer the butt of company jokes and even began a monogamous relationship with a man from a completely different field. This was a complete change from her previous dating patterns and ethical behavior.

It is not particularly difficult to change a belief, unless you program yourself to consider it an insurmountable task. A simple refocusing of your attention through self-hypnosis can effect a major change in your beliefs, as long as you are willing and motivated to permit this change to take place.

This system is a natural one that utilizes a technique that is a part of our normal functioning. Hypnosis (all of which is self-hypnosis) is this natural technique. We exhibit hypnosis whenever we daydream, watch television, read, listen to music and dream during our sleep cycle. Out of every twenty-four hour day, seven hours are spent in natural self-hypnosis!

Without the benefit of this alpha brain wave level we call hypnosis, our life would end. This natural relaxation and destressing component of our brain's physiology is as crucial to our survival as our heart beat.

It is our inner mental and emotional states of mind that create our personal world of unique people, challenges, joys, sorrows, friends and loved ones. You must learn to change your inner world if you expect the outer universe to become more pleasant and financially rewarding.

To master this art of changing the outer world in which you function to increase abundance by applying time tested principles of metaphysics, you simply need to examine and alter those beliefs that sabotage this goal. When you personally apply the techniques presented in this book, you will observe the direct connection between what you focus on in your mind and the events that are subsequently observed.

Only then will you begin to comprehend that each one of us are beings with unlimited abilities and potentials that are just

waiting to be discovered. The thoughts in our mind are not inert substances stored in the physical brain. These ideas are composed of energy as real as electricity.

Your imagination resonates with your ideas. Your future experience will be the outcome of what you imagine, think, and feel in the present moment. Your current experience is the outcome of what you imagined, thought, and felt in the past "present" moments. If you want to create a future significantly different from your current experience, you must restructure your framework of ideas.

The mechanism of instituting these changes involves three steps. Finding what your ideas are represents the initial step. The second phase is selecting which specific thoughts you want to make a part of your reality, and which ones you choose to delete from your awareness. Finally, reprogramming your subconscious by using self-hypnosis will incorporate this new mental climate and mind set into your awareness.

It is always difficult to convince a person set in their ways that what they are doing just doesn't work. This is especially true with ruthless and narrow-minded businessmen. Frederick was such an example.

Frederick came to my office several years ago complaining of various psychosomatic disorders. He described digestive problems, insomnia, headaches, compulsive eating and alcohol abuse. He was an arrogant, cold and ruthless businessman, who prided himself on his ability to manipulate and take advantage of others.

This was not an easy case to begin. I only agreed to see Frederick upon his demonstrating to me that he was motivated to mend his ways. He sounded quite sincere and was most impressed by the training I provided to one of his employees in assisting that particular gentleman in overcoming some of the very issues that currently plagued Frederick.

I completed my work with Frederick in five three hour sessions. This is my typical program for out of state patients. He promised to keep me posted about his progress during the coming months. It took fifteen months to receive a call from Frederick relating his progress, resolution of his psychosomatic problems and a very interesting story of his application of the principles of karmic capitalism.

What Frederick was not aware of was that I had received a call from one of his business associates, a man named Vance, just four months earlier relating this very same anecdote.

Vance had a contractual relationship with Frederick on a very lucrative option to purchase a piece of commercial property. This contract was about to lapse and Vance needed additional time to secure the funds needed to exercise this option. Knowing Frederick's reputation, Vance expected a rejection of an extension on this option.

To Vance's surprise, Frederick agreed to an extension with no penalties. Six months later Vance bought this property and paid Frederick a bonus over and above the purchase price as an expression of his appreciation. In addition, Vance referred several of his clients and friends to the now trim, healthy and more fulfilled Frederick. Karmic capitalism can work wonders with the most resistant people.

The universe does work in mysterious ways. When you access your Higher Self on a regular basis and practice an ethical and empowering lifestyle, rewards originate from unexpected sources. A case in point happened to me in 1989. I owned a house in Maryland that was rented to a couple on an option to purchase basis.

Living in Los Angeles 3,000 miles away from my investment does incur some disadvantages. Fortunately, I have good friends whom I have known for many years that function as agents in my real estate dealings. Paul is one such friend.

Paul managed this building for me when I moved from Maryland to Los Angeles early in 1989. This couple had lived in my rental property for two years and were excellent tenants. A job transfer out of state made it impossible for them to consummate the purchase of this house.

As the rent was always paid on time and this building did not require repairs, Paul did not have to do anything to this property upon its vacancy. When the tenants moved, Paul rerented this house immediately and all went well.

The next communication I received from Paul concerning this house occurred three months later. An offer to buy this house was made by the new tenants who had lived in that building for less than three months!

Apparently, this couple knew of my honest reputation and trusted one of my houses as being a solid purchase, versus taking a chance on the open market. They had spoken to another family that bought one of my houses two years before. I negotiated a sales price five percent below the current market value. They immediately accepted and took title to their dream house eight weeks later.

Paul later asked me why I just didn't sell this house at the market value. I informed him that since I wasn't using a realtor, I didn't feel right charging them the equivalent of the commission such an agent would have charged me. This brought about a laugh from Paul as he said to me, "you and your karmic capitalism."

One result of this price savings for my buyers was several thousands of dollars in interest to the bank, in addition to a reduced mortgage payment. This sent out a positive energy signal to the universe which amply rewarded me the following year when this very same couple referred an investor to me who purchased several of my tax lien certificates on buildings that were too much in need of repair for me to fix up. Instead of writing them off as a loss, I received my investment back in full, along with twenty-four percent interest. Me and my karmic capitalism – indeed!

Paul's story is also relevant in discussing karmic capitalism. In 1985 he was working for the State of Maryland and miserable with his job. I offered him a fifty percent partnership in properties he would purchase for me at foreclosure auctions.

He agreed and was the successful bidder on a building that year that sold the following spring netting me about $12,000.00 in profit. His share was the same, but he desperately needed $7,000 at the end of 1985. I advanced him these funds, and this allowed him to consummate another business deal which enabled him to quit his state job and enter into a far more rewarding field that he still is active in.

In addition, Paul was able to make a commitment to his girlfriend and today is a rather successful businessman. He feels eternally indebted to me, much against my insistence that all I was doing was being a karmic capitalist. Me and my karmic capitalism.

An excellent example of karmic capitalism involves a struggling entrepreneur named Jesse I met several years ago. Although he was never a patient, he purchased several of my tapes on self-hypnosis (the scripts of these will be presented in chapter 5) and expressed interest in an investment vehicle I use in the State of Maryland known as tax lien certificates.

A tax lien certificate is a lien placed on a property when the owner of record fails to pay their property taxes timely. The investor purchases these investments at a public auction. One of two things will then happen. Either the owner pays the investor all monies he or she advanced at the auction plus twenty-four percent interest, or the investor forecloses and takes title to this property, wiping out all mortgages and previous liens.

As a major player in this market since the 1980's, I own hundreds of these certificates. Jesse lacked the several thousand dollars required to purchase the certificates from me. He played my superconscious mind tape and was advised to propose a sweat equity exchange for a fifty percent ownership in the property.

His offer would involve him fixing up the buildings himself (sweat equity) and paying me no funds. My responsibility would consist of splitting any net profits from the eventual sale of this house.

I accessed my own Higher Self to confirm my positive approach to Jesse's offer. I liked his energy as expressed by our conversations, and admired his spunk and willingness to work hard toward a future goal. Needless to say, my superconscious mind tap highly recommended this deal.

Several months later this building was sold. In the interim period of time Jesse rented this home out and received ten percent of the rent as a management fee. When the building did sell, Jesse's share of the profits was over $7,000.00.

This represented more money than Jesse had seen in his entire life. He later purchased two other of my tax lien certificates outright with his new bankroll. I received my twenty-four percent interest, and Jesse made several thousand dollars on the eventual sale of each of these fixer-uppers.

The reason why Jesse simply didn't attend one of the city's auctions is that it requires hundreds of thousands of dollars of purchases of tax lien certificates to eventually end up with the building, as the great majority of them pay off. Jesse's initial sweat equity paved the way for his earning quite a bit of money through this little known investment vehicle.

This represented a true win-win-win situation. I won by receiving a twenty-four percent return on my investment. Jesse benefited by being able to earn a lot of money with no financial investment (he simply didn't have the money to buy these certificates at first). Finally, the city won by receiving its delinquent property taxes. You will find karmic capitalism, more often than not, results in a win-win-win conclusion.

SUMMARIZING UP-1, UP-2 AND UP-3

Currently, we are somewhere in the middle of a shift from UP-1 to UP-3. If you accept the UP-3 belief (as do all karmic capitalists), then we are all one with nature and in harmony with the universe. It is our false beliefs that create disharmony and problems. All of this is correctable by simply altering these dysfunctional beliefs. We will discuss this concept in greater detail in chapter 4.

Karmic capitalism works because of our perception of the world. As more and more businesses come on board to karmic capitalism, institutions will be more person-centered. This further reinforces the concept of being connected to each other and to the universe. We must establish a balance between the masculine and feminine influences on business.

Masculine business forces have traditionally been aggressiveness, competition, manipulative technology and reductionist scientific thought. Opposing these forces are the feminine influences of intuitiveness, nurturing and cooperation. This male dominated paradigm has persisted for about 5,000 years. It simply must be modified to a more partnership approach, and that is what karmic capitalism on the corporate level is all about.

When karmic capitalism is fully activated globally, we will see a phasing out of a consumer approach in favor of paradigms encouraging a true form of self-reliance, empowerment, creativity and liberation of the spirit. This will be accompanied by an elimination of cynicism, fatalism, win-lose mentalities, submission to external authority and self-denigration. What will result is an increase in autonomy, productivity, pride and self-realization in the workplace.

In other words, we no longer will be obsessed with having more – we will want simply to be more. Karmic capitalism in the corporate world will place more emphasis on awakening to the realization that one has been imprisoned by "buying into" a set of beliefs which, once this is realized, one need not accept. A complete discussion on corporate karmic capitalism is presented in chapters 7 and 8.

CHAPTER 3

THE ROLE OF CONSCIOUSNESS IN ABUNDANCE

Our individual level of spirituality is expressed by the presence of our soul in the universe. We have a three-dimensional consciousness in the form of our conscious mind proper (the ego or defense mechanisms), the subconscious (soul) and the superconscious (Higher Self).

Each of these three components has its own level of awareness. The ego is only within our consciousness for the term of our current life. It then disappears following physical death. Our soul is permanent in the form of energy, and survives physical death, hopefully more evolved as a result of our earth sojourn. Finally, we have the Higher Self. This energy originates from the God energy, and is the only part of our awareness that is perfect. Many refer to this superconscious mind energy as the "divine spark within us."

To attain a broader appreciation of these various levels of consciousness, I highly recommend the superconscious mind tap exercise. This simple technique allows us to globally assess the universe from a far more objective, yet spiritual perspective.

Through the presence of our Higher Self, we have within us a vehicle for the manifestation of the God energy. The soul is God's idea manifested in a higher plane of consciousness, and we are the soul's idea manifested in the three-dimensional plane of consciousness. Just as a physicist discovers energy as the basis of matter (Einstein demonstrated that matter and energy may be converted to one another with his famous $E=MC2$), the energy in the form of electromagnetic radiation that constitutes our soul is a microcosm of the universe as a whole.

We are all innately given a will to live, along with the will to evolve spiritually to become a functional part of the universe's design. Intelligence, love, compassion and other qualities we possess are merely a means to an end. The end is ascension to rejoin God.

The world that we live in is created by our consciousness as a form of exercise in creativity. We use our consciousness to manifest our physical and psychic reality, and to test our beliefs by creating a variety of situations that test our karmic muscle. This reality is constantly being molded by our thoughts, feelings and actions. We create our own reality through the strength and intensity of these factors.

The earth plane in which we currently function is a classroom, a laboratory of sorts, where our souls may create and respond to certain lessons in the form of experiences. The ultimate purpose of these exercises is always the same: spiritual growth.

When you finally do acknowledge this paradigm, you have attained a certain level of spiritual unfoldment. We now must add a fourth dimension to complete this paradigm (there are actually several other dimensions, but that would require a book in itself). The eternal now of spaceless, timeless, energy-based reality represents this fourth dimension.

This eternal now has no concept of past or future. Everything is happening at the same moment. There is no "cause and effect" as we have been brainwashed to believe. It is only through mindfulness behavior and accessing our Higher elf that we can get a glimpse of this fourth dimension.

Fear and anger prevent the average person from this experience. Since fear is the memory of past pain projected into the future, and anger is the revisiting of past pain, this pain creates an energy imbalance. The low spiritual energy of the ego throws the higher vibrational rate of evolvement of the soul out of alignment. If we don't request assistance from our Higher Self, fear enters and contaminates our reality. That is why fear is the most important obstacle to our soul's growth, and why I keep emphasizing the superconscious mind tap to connect with our Higher Self.

We can gain even a more comprehensive glimpse of this eternal now by exploring our dream state. I am not referring to interpreting these nightly movies. What I do mean is the Rapid Eye Movement (REM) state we commonly call dreaming is a voyage to the Astral Plane, where all time is simultaneous and a four-dimensional awareness exists. My book Dream Your Problems Away has several dozen exercises to introduce you to the fascinating dreamworld universe.

These awareness levels function as boundaries to our reality perception. My theory is that devoid of these boundaries we, as imperfect souls, would be retarded in our motivation to grow spiritually. What we often classify as limitations may very well be the spark that ignites our spiritual unfoldment.

Making a commitment to living life fully, clears away reactive, fear-driven motivation and exposes the roots of your own true essence. Being inspired and spiritual is our natural state. Attuning ourselves to our Higher Self level of consciousness facilitates our movement towards perfection faster than any other mechanism I have investigated. Never underestimate the universe's bliss and eternal rewards.

As children growing up, most of us have fantasies of what we want to be when we are adults. The problem is that a tremendous amount of energy is wasted trying to fulfill these dreams, or those of our parents.

The very jobs that most people settle for do not allow for creative expression, meaningful contributions or enough money to impress people in our materialistic society. This results in moving from job to job and from career to career. No position, no boss and no career can fulfill your karmic purpose.

You have the option of being among the privileged few on this planet who can move beyond issues of personal survival and begin to explore expanded dimensions of your potential by maintaining a daily communication with your Higher Self. Use your God-given consciousness to effect this change.

Today we are witnessing a long awaited search for inner knowledge and the ultimate truth. This personal search has led to greater interest in astrology, psychology, psychic phenomena, parapsychology, spiritualism, and theosophy, among others.

This idea that our subconscious mind represents a source of wisdom and enlightenment, and a true linkage with the spiritual dimensions can be traced back to Plotinus in the 2nd century, A.D. and Saint Augustine in the 4th century, A.D., both of whom stated that consciousness is present in all matter. Matter is molded by consciousness through the energy associated with our thoughts and beliefs. As we shift our awareness to higher states of consciousness, we move into a realm of joy and peace. Everything exists in these higher states of consciousness as a field of energy.

Although the energy in the universe expresses itself in a specific physical form, we have the potential to alter this manifestation at other times depending on our beliefs. All of the information concerning our past, present and future is to be found in the fourth dimension of consciousness. We can access this data by communicating with our Higher Self through the superconscious mind tap presented in chapter 2, for example.

Throughout our daily lives our five senses and beliefs limit our exposure to only the three-dimensional consciousness. Most of the time it is only two-dimensional, since most people ignore their Higher Self.

The universe of the fourth dimension is difficult to grasp due to our limiting beliefs. Although Einstein demonstrated that energy and mass are interchangeable (E=MC2), a world where space and time merge in a single continuum, and one based totally on energy, is beyond most individual's comprehension.

Consciousness has been studied since ancient times. The phrase "know thyself" was etched in stone above the entrance to the temple of Apollo in Delphi, Greece. The Upanishads refer to this as the "highest light." The ascetic life of contemplation and study was used by many to understand the meaning of life. The problem with this approach became evident when these individuals attempted to apply their insights in their daily life.

When you leave your sanctuary and move into the real world, your inner peace shatters in an instant if you have not fully integrated the insights of self-knowledge into your life. This can only be accomplished by somehow accessing your Higher Self. The superconscious mind tap I keep alluding to is not the only way to do this, it's just the most efficient. By establishing an audience with your Higher Self, you will truly "know yourself."

We must always remember that the body is just a vehicle of the mind in three-dimensional consciousness. This mind is the true expression of our being. Our brain is the part of the physical body that controls and coordinates the autonomic and immune systems. The brain is not the storehouse of our memories.

The work of Karl Lashley demonstrated that surgically removing various parts of the brain of rats trained to perform a variety of tasks did not inhibit these abilities. In other words, no matter what portion of the brain he removed, the rats could still repeat the tasks they had learned! Lashley concluded that memories are not located in any specific brain sites. Therefore, it must be the mind, not the brain, that stores our memories.

The mind cannot be located in space and time and cannot be perceived by our senses. The mind's principal attribute is consciousness. It is our connection to higher states of consciousness in the form of our Higher Self that facilitates our spiritual growth through reincarnation. Physical death is merely a change in awareness, during which our conscious mind dies and the soul migrates to the Astral Plane and eventually to the Soul Plane to select its future life. This mechanism involves traversing the fourth-dimension consciousness.

The soul or subconscious functions as our life force. The spirit energy of the soul leaves with it at the moment of death. This results in a loss of cohesiveness of the physical body and its disintegration and return to basic chemical elements. This mind is the only part of our consciousness that retains our memories following our physical death.

51

In Peaceful Transition I describe at length how reports of patients who had near-death experiences (NDEs) demonstrate awareness of data they couldn't possibly have derived from their five senses, including the ability to see into the future! They also describe a lack of change of awareness from the trip originating from the Physical Plane to the Astral Plane and returning to the physical world.

Is it mere coincidence that those who have experienced an NDE are almost always transformed? They become happier, more optimistic and easygoing, and less concerned about material possessions. Their capacity to love expands enormously and parallels an increased interest in spirituality. The experience occurs in the fourth dimension of consciousness. Perhaps it is because they have been in direct contact with their Higher Self. In any event, does this not sound like karmic capitalism?

Theoretically, when we reach higher states of consciousness, we can connect with other souls, while still maintaining our individuality. This affords us a tremendous opportunity to utilize a communication with our Higher Self to bring about abundance goals, while at the same time continuing with our spiritual unfoldment.

Is our level of consciousness directly proportional to the degree of fragmentation we allow into our believes about whom we are? David Bohm, the physicist suggests that everything in the universe is part of a continuum. Humans, and all matter, are reducible to energy forms. Our tendency to fragment the world and ignore the dynamic interconnectedness of all things is responsible for all our problems. This results in an inability to see the big picture by viewing all obstacles in isolation. We treat symptoms instead of causes. Consider modern medicine as an example with its obsession with drugs to mask symptoms. It is only through accessing our Higher Self that we will be capable of seeing the forest through the trees.

Consciousness teaches us that only when we give unconditionally to the universe do we receive in return an equal or greater gift. If your intention is to get something that you feel you lack, you always repel what you want. Whatever you give out unconditionally is what you attract. You push away what you crave, and attract what you freely give away. These simple words can go a long way in removing your fears and raising your consciousness.

If you only seek power, money, or status, you often find that you will sacrifice your family life and relationships. Power, money, and status are also forms of energy. As you try to fill the void you feel inside by pulling these toward you, they tend to escape you. To get them you sacrifice your integrity and principles. In the end you find only pain and sorrow.

Our consciousness gives the events in your life all the meaning they have for you. The emotional content of any experience is based on the set of beliefs that you have about that experience. The emotions we express are only an interpretation of reality, not reality itself. Through our consciousness we choose how to interpret the events based on our beliefs about the situation. Your emotions, thoughts, and behavior reflect your beliefs.

As souls we are always responsible for creating our realities. We are never the victims of circumstance. The cause lies within us. Accepting responsibility for your life means recognizing that, at some level, you create your own reality. Our choices are simply that we can either be responsible, or we can be victims. The first choice gives you the power to change your life, while the second puts you at the mercy of others.

CREATIVITY

Our consciousness is very much involved with our creative talents. Truly groundbreaking concepts are rare, but focusing our awareness on innovation allows our Higher Self to present to our subconscious a logical combination of two or more existing ideas that results in a new concept. This is my definition of creativity.

The key here is to develop innovative applications, not try to come up with a completely new concept. Let others try to reinvent the wheel. In the meantime, work on developing a better hubcap.

Another way to be creative is to find what is called a "high concept." This is a Hollywood term (you can tell where I reside) for a valuable idea that is both marketable and quickly understood.

I suggest you read as much as you can using as many diverse sources as time allows on a variety of subjects. When you observe the same idea appearing in several magazines and newspapers, consider it a candidate for a high concept.

It is important to brainstorm with others well outside your area of expertise. Listen to the opinions and directions of others whom you respect, especially if they are fellow karmic capitalists. Try to adopt ideas with a good track record to contemporary markets. Some things never change. Always consider other merchandise possibilities from your main idea to maximize its commercial attraction and profit potential. I will present a self-hypnosis exercise on improving creativity in chapter 5.

HOLDING GRUDGES

Our consciousness and emotional state is negatively affected when we bear grudges. The karmic capitalist learns quickly to eliminate this tendency by practicing forgiveness. It is little wonder that most religions encourage the process of forgiveness.

Most of us truly want to forgive others, but something gets in the way and distracts us. The physical, mental and emotional energy expended in fostering a grudge often leaves us angry, depressed and obsessive.

The more anger we experience within, the more stress we're under. The inability to let go of hurt makes it harder to trust or feel close to others. Your grudge can infect your family—or prime social network—forcing everyone to choose sides and establish loyalties. Secrets and spite take the place of love and caring. It is now impossible to practice karmic capitalism.

Forgiving is an internal process that releases the spiritual energy required to banish these ills and fill relationships with warmth. Don't be surprised to observe your creativity improving at the same time.

The first step in forgiveness is identifying and overcoming the fears, false beliefs and misconceptions that make it difficult to forgive. Here are some false, unconstructive beliefs that block us from forgiving easily:

1. I am showing a sign of weakness by forgiving.

In reality, a great deal of character is required to be strong and assertive enough to be able to express one's feelings directly, rather than lying or being "politically correct."

2. By forgiving I will be letting the offending party get away with something.

What you are doing is establishing the unacceptability of the wrongful behavior in the future. You can take more assertive actions if this circumstance repeats itself.

3. If I forgive, I'll have to trust the other person, and I'm afraid I'll be hurt again.

Trust must always be earned. When you forgive you free yourself from an uncomfortable emotion, nothing more. Let them earn your trust, but be open to them getting their act together.

4. It is phony to act forgiving if I don't really feel it.

You would be surprised how fast your emotions will follow suit to your "phony" actions when you forgive. Access your Higher Self to facilitate this process.

5. I can't forgive until I forget.

When you discharge the negative emotions attached to a negative act, you will quickly initiate the process of forgetting.

Karmic capitalism implies that we give the precise meaning to events in our life that we choose to. Do not take the stance of victim or use excusitis. You make your karmic bed so be careful where your soul rests.

CHAPTER 4

BELIEFS THAT PROMOTE KARMIC CAPITALISM

"Whatever you ask in prayer, believe
that you receive it and you will."

Mark 11:234

CORE BELIEFS

No matter who we are, there are certain basic beliefs that characterize all of us. These core beliefs may vary greatly depending on our experiences and what we accept, but they are there as a framework nonetheless. These core beliefs can be stated as follows:

1.   Optimism versus pessimism. Is your cup half empty (pessimist), half full (optimist) or is it overflowing (karmic capitalist)? You can easily define your orientation to this core belief by noting your initial response to a difficult situation.

The pessimist whines and complains and says, "Just my luck" or "I should've known this was going to happen." Developing a positive attitude is necessary to become a karmic capitalist. You need to move beyond mere optimism to true karmic capitalistic mentality.

Developing a positive mind set requires assessing any situation objectively and formulating a creative and constructive resolution to this issue. All "problems" in life are looked upon as opportunities for learning and a training ground to exercise your karmic capitalistic muscle.

Affirmations
- I create my reality with complete positivity.
- I enjoy my life and create abundance daily.

- I succeed in all my endeavors.
- I love life and never compromise my ethics.
- Everyone I come into contact with teaches me something useful.
- I always expect the best from others and the universe.

2. Self-worth beliefs. Each of us has a self-image that we create from our thoughts and experiences. Granted we often are raised in an environment of criticism and low self-esteem, but you don't have to allow this dysfunctional background to affect the rest of your life.

If you do not love yourself and truly, in your "heart-of-hearts" feel that you are worthy of success and happiness, these goals will elude you. Your self-image must be universally high to become a karmic capitalist. It is not sufficient to feel confident at your chosen profession, but a failure in your personal relationships.

You cannot feel wonderful about yourself spiritually, but dislike your body. A high self-worth concerning your sexuality accompanied by a resignation in your inability to attain abundance doesn't work either.

Affirmations
- I love myself.
- I deserve the best the universe offers me.
- My soul is a component of God.
- I can accomplish anything I set my mind to.
- I am competent and confident at any undertaking.
- I am worthy of love, both giving and receiving it.

3. Passing the karmic buck. It is quite common to shift the blame for something you participated in that didn't work out. The karmic capitalist must take responsibility for his or her actions, not just the successful ones. Self-responsibility is an important core belief.

We always have a choice as to how we can respond to life's opportunities. By accepting self-responsibility and learning, growing and subsequently benefiting from each of life's tests, we eliminate the need to repeat the same mistakes over and over again. Once we successfully learn a karmic lesson, we are no longer exposed to this same test. This is a basic law of metaphysics.

Affirmations
- I take full responsibility for everything I do.
- I always choose to grow.
- My mind creates my present circumstances and custom designs my future.
- I control my future, not the past or some other person or institution.

4.   Change versus sameness. Most people are conservative in their beliefs and prefer the stability and security of sameness versus change. Becoming anxious and stressed at any form of change is a core belief that must be replaced in order to attain the status of karmic capitalist.

We are brainwashed to think that stability is a natural law. Change is the basic rule in the universe. The seasons change, we age, technology completely reorients our behavior and attempts to improve our lives and so on. The Ying/Yang philosophy of the Chinese illustrate this concept well.

Today our society is changing at a more rapid pace than ever before. Those that refuse to keep up with this ever-changing world will be left behind. The karmic capitalist is always on the forefront of change.

Affirmations
•   I am open to changes brought on by the universe.
•   Changes are good and they result in spiritual growth.
•   I flow with the universe's changes and always consider them opportunities for learning.

5.   The universe is good or evil. This belief stems from theological brainwashing. If you believe that the universe is evil and only religion can save your soul, you will never become a karmic capitalist. Empowerment, not codependency on a dogma, characterizes a karmic capitalist. Interestingly enough, my experience has shown that those patients of mine who believe the universe is good and trust in it, act with a greater sense of security and empowerment than those who do not.

People who distrust the universe must continually protect themselves from those who would prey on them or "rip them off." They spend their entire life fearful of everyone and quite lonely. The energy we send out will always come back to us. This is another basic metaphysical law.

Affirmation
•   I put my faith and trust in the universe.
•   I believe people are good, as is the universe.
•   I create my own universe daily and enjoy the process.
•   There is nothing I cannot do, as the universe provides me with all of the raw materials for spiritual growth.

As long as you are willing to be completely honest with yourself, your beliefs are readily accessible. Simply monitor your thoughts at various times during the day. Observe the various trains of thought on which you seem to focus. What beliefs do these thoughts represent?

As a simple exercise carry a notepad with you throughout your day and jot down any dominant thought that crosses your mind. Do not attempt to analyze these thoughts or classify them, merely record the raw data. At the end of the day place these thoughts in categories such as positive, negative, intuitive, situational and reactive. This will give you a good idea as to the types of thoughts that are running through your mind daily.

You can modify this approach by writing down your ideas on a specific area such as finances. Write a mini-essay on your attitude toward money and financial plans for the next six months. Try to discover whether you are holding onto any ideas that work against karmic capitalism. Pay special attention to those thoughts that foster this approach.

We develop beliefs from three sources. The society into which we are raised is our initial source of these beliefs. Interactions with those that we respect and consider close, such as parents, teachers and other role models, represent a second source for our beliefs. The most spiritual and significant source is what our soul came into our body with from previous lifetimes. This demonstrates a karmic source of our beliefs.

The actual beliefs we adopt are a sum total of the experiences we have, the angst of society and the effects of our communication with the world, along with our Higher Self contacts. They are not necessarily based on fact, nor are they an accurate depiction of the reality systems of our fellow citizens.

A common acceptance of certain paradigms promulgated by society may be the basis of most of our beliefs. This is a dangerous tendency, as it fosters brainwashing and limits spiritual growth. No matter where you go on this planet, you will encounter systems of thought based on certain beliefs. Our entire world operates on the basis of individual and collective belief systems. Without beliefs nothing would have meaning.

Karmic capitalism cannot be achieved without an all-around growth process. We do have control over our beliefs, so if you are dissatisfied with your life or simply want to attain abundance, an alteration of your present beliefs is in order.

Repressed emotions can result from accepting the limited belief system of how you "should" act or what you "should" feel in certain situations. There are emotions you may disapprove of, think are inappropriate or, worse yet, fear.

There is no issue, challenge or problem that cannot be dealt with in a positive and empowering manner. Allowing yourself to feel the full range of your emotions means acknowledging and feeling whatever you are feeling and letting your emotions flow naturally. It is easy to trace the origin of a belief to an emotion. Allow yourself to fully experience an emotion and then trace it to the thoughts and beliefs that are associated with it Altering the beliefs will automatically change the emotions.

Beliefs are often accepted by us as a result of us being exposed to these ideas from authority figures and role models. Parents, teachers, sports figures and other celebrities can have a great effect on shaping our beliefs. Many such beliefs have unfortunately been accepted by us without the benefit of our best critical judgment.

We need new criteria to change these beliefs. Basing your selection of beliefs to accept by repetition of old patterns of behavior simply will not facilitate spiritual growth. If this technique didn't work in the past, what makes you think it is going to work now?

A new system has to be incorporated that rejects ideas that downgrade your worth or power. Anything that works contrary to your desires to become a karmic capitalist needs to be replaced by more productive beliefs. Listen to your Higher Self. Trust it. Let it be your guide, along with your intellect, when making your choice of new beliefs.

For example, if you believe it's hard to make and save money, alter this belief by stating that it is only difficult to attract abundance if you don't have a game plan. Now use your mind to devise a game plan and begin a new belief paradigm.

As you practice this system of changing beliefs, always remember that this is an ongoing process. The beliefs on which you choose to focus now may not serve your purposes at some future point; then you can select new ones.

CHANGING OUR BELIEFS

We program ourselves negatively in a variety of ways by using a dysfunctional form of self-hypnosis. Our mind is constantly fed suggestions through the media or social circles informing us that we are fat or fit, rich or poor, healthy or sick, or something in between.

Dramatic self-improvements can be initiated through the use of self-hypnosis by changing the focus of our inner dialogues to more positive suggestions about ourselves. This is far more than mere positive thinking. Positive thinking alone acts on the will power alone, and is doomed to fail unless constantly reinforced.

Self-hypnosis, on the other hand, reprograms the subconscious and effects a permanent change. Constant reinforcement is not necessary. We can literally reprogram our subconscious to believe whatever it is that we want to believe. The best way to do this is with tapes. To learn how to make your own self-hypnosis tapes from the scripts that are presented in this book, I suggest my book New Age Hypnosis. This book instructs you step by step how to produce quickly and inexpensively your own self-hypnosis tapes.

Throughout our daily lives we are continually hypnotizing ourselves to believe what we currently believe. Changing beliefs is not fundamentally difficult. It is only when you are reluctant to relinquish old beliefs and gamble on replacing them with new ones that difficulties are encountered. Your defense mechanisms are conditioned to be skeptical about a belief that runs contrary to your conventional thinking. The evidence will follow, but only after you have altered your belief.

It may, at this time, seem unlikely that new opportunities for abundance will surface in your life by simply reprogramming the subconscious to alter its beliefs. A little faith in this system is required to begin this process. You must act on these challenges with the new positively programmed you in order to materialize them.

The most demanding aspect of karmic capitalism is that you are asked to exert the greatest investment of energy, discipline, faith and commitment when you have often no feedback that this paradigm will work for you. A quantum leap, or leap of faith, is required in any spiritually based system for progress to have a chance. You must defer gratification and the usual way of doing things as part of your discipline to initiate this approach. The demands of karmic capitalism are great, but the rewards are even greater.

Fear is a very destructive emotion that will grind to a halt any advances you may make as a karmic capitalist. You must overcome all of your fears to change your life and attain abundance.

Fear-based principles often mask the fear itself, but are still destructive to your ability to accomplish your definition of success. Review this list of fear mentalities and see how many of them apply to your life now:

- Never admit a mistake because others will think you are incompetent.
- Alter the truth to preserve the feelings of someone you work with.
- Assume colleagues are after your job, or are trying to sabotage your career.
- Shift the blame for something you are responsible for onto someone else.
- Always make sure you receive credit for something you do outside of the office for fear people won't like or respect you.

- Manipulate others to do something for you to avoid rejection.
- Never ask for help at the office.
- Distrust other workers for fear that they will hurt you in some way.
- Always try and fit in so that you will be accepted.
- Never show any sign of being imperfect.
- Become anxious anytime the boss calls you into his or her office.
- Act in a cynical manner concerning your standing and growth potential with your company.

As an example of this principle consider a business opportunity that presents itself to you. What are your options? You can refuse to become involved and watch someone else capitalize on this venture. Another possibility is to seek an advisor or partner for this deal. Thirdly, you can research this investment and take it on yourself. Your ultimate choice depends on your belief system and self-image.

Once you have made any needed adjustments in your belief systems, you will have to act on the adjusted beliefs in order to materialize your goal of becoming financially independent. It now becomes time to back up your goals with consistent practice, just as you would when learning any other skill. Fear of failure, however, must be eliminated from your belief system.

Resistance to change is an issue that often surfaces when changing beliefs. Change is something we all have to deal with, but actively manipulating your reality means accelerating change. It is important to trust your Higher Self. This perfect part of your consciousness will assist in removing any fears. It is crucial that you learn to trust in your inner wisdom and overcome these previous limiting beliefs.

The ability to consciously manipulate the contents of your mind is an invaluable skill that can be used to achieve success with any business enterprise, and any other aspect of your life. Here is a simple exercise that will train you to alter your beliefs and develop new ones:

Select some areas from the following list. For each area, follow the six steps. Work on one area at a time.

Your power	Your body
Men	Your worth
Women	Aging
Money	Your community
Your children	Yourself
Health	Work
Your intuition	Relationships
Your spouse	Sex

1.   Describe thoroughly your feelings, thoughts and beliefs in relation to the specific topics you chose.

2.   Prepare a concise one or two sentence statement reflecting your belief.

3.   Place any belief you consider limiting on a separate page.

4.   Prepare a new positive belief to replace the limiting ones. This new belief could be the complete opposite of your previous belief.

5.   Again prepare a concise one or two sentence statement (affirmative) describing this new positive belief. Use the present tense as if the new belief were already true. For example:

I am a confident, empowered and successful businessperson.

I attract associates and clients into my life that reflect my high ethical code and quality orientation to life.

6.   Use the superconscious mind tap script and repeat your affirmation statements to yourself. Do this with conviction, and act as if each and every one of these statements were true today.

When following an affirmation the following guidelines will be of assistance.

- State it in positive terms.
- Be very specific and brief.
- Word it in the as if it already exists mode.
- Center it around yourself, not others.
- Write it down.

ABUNDANCE BELIEFS

Our beliefs about money play a major role in our ability to both earn and keep it. The following three classes of monetary beliefs help determine your current mind set about abundance:

1.   Money is either good or evil. If you feel money is evil, your ability to accumulate it will be quite limited. The reverse is also true. In reality, money is neither good nor evil – it's neutral. What we do to earn and keep it may very well be good or evil, but not the concept of money itself.

Money can be used to control and humiliate others. It may be transformed into healing (buying health services), entertainment or food and shelter. It is our attitudes and actions that determine the ultimate effect money has on our lives.

2.   Poverty consciousness versus prosperity consciousness. A poverty consciousness is based on the belief that there never is enough money (no

matter how much you have). This fear of scarcity is both a denial of creative potential and low self-worth belief.

The belief that the universe continually provides us with abundance and we are quite capable of harvesting this abundance is prosperity consciousness. One dominant theme of this healthier belief system is that there will always be enough money to meet our requirements in life, and we have the ability to earn more when we deem it necessary.

3.   More money is better versus less money is better. Only you can decide the correct amount of money to acquire. You create your reality, and as a karmic capitalist there is no need to place limits on your ability to attain abundance. Although society constantly judges people on how much or little money they possess, don't fall into this trap. "Judge ye not, lest you be judged."

The following are limiting beliefs about money and affirmations to change these beliefs:

Limiting Belief: My life partner earns more money than me. I have no right to spend their income.

Affirmation: We have a true partnership. I supplement our life together with my energy, domestic work and love. I have as much right to spend this money as my partner.

Limiting Belief: I must sacrifice my creative and spiritual components of my life to earn money.

Affirmation: I utilize my creative talents and maintain my ethics in all professional pursuits. My spirituality grows with each business day.

Limiting Belief: The more money I make, the more people will exhibit jealousy and dislike me.

Affirmation: My world will be such that only those quality souls secure and spiritual enough to appreciate my professional success will enter into my life.

Limiting Belief: It is too difficult and stressful to earn the kind of money I desire.

Affirmation: I am a karmic capitalist, whose spirituality and confidence allows me to effortlessly earn as much money as I desire.

Limiting Belief: Earning a lot of money will make me obsessive and unhappy.

Affirmation: I maintain a perfect physical, mental, emotional and spiritual balance as I attain abundance.

Limiting Belief: Attaining abundance means becoming stuck in a boring and repetitive business.

Affirmation: I access my Higher Self and constantly exercise creativity, passion and variety as I attain abundance.

Another factor in effecting a change in beliefs is the intensity of your desire, or internal motivation. This is the key to truly altering a previously dysfunction belief. By being properly directed you can easily use your natural imagination and creativity to alter your mind set and create what you want in life, such as abundance.

If your mental climate is either too limiting or clouded by fear, you will find it impossible to change previous belief systems. The biggest obstacle to both change and any form of spiritual growth is fear. The superconscious mind script or tape will assist you in overcoming this all important obstacle.

Here is another exercise to help you in examining your current beliefs and fears. I suggest you practice the superconscious mind self hypnosis exercise before beginning this exercise:

1.   Get comfortable and take several long, slow deep breaths. Say 20, 20, 20 to yourself and relax.

2.   As you consider the questions I am about to present, allow your answers to come from your subconscious. Refrain from analyzing them, or making some form of judgment.

3.   Take your time with this exercise and always be completely honest with yourself. Examine the complete range of beliefs corresponding to each question. If you discover that you hold conflicting ideas in a certain area, write down both sides. Let your thoughts flow, and write as much as you want.

4.   When you are finished with the first subject area and questions, clear your mind and proceed with the next. Continue until you have covered all of the areas.

Questions

1.   Are you uneasy about becoming financially independent? Elaborate your answer and cite specific examples.

2.   What education, talents, experiences or other qualifications do you have that will help you to attain your financial goals?

3.   What factors, real or imaginary, are preventing you from reaching your financial goals?

4.   How comfortable or safe do you feel in your life at this time?

5.   Is there any single factor or factors that represents a threat to your attaining abundance?

6.   What are your fears in general? List possible ways to overcome each and every one of these fears.

7.   How do you feel about spirituality? Are you afraid to utilize self-hypnosis and superconscious mind taps to facilitate your spiritual growth and the attainment of abundance?

8.   How strong is your desire to become financially independent?

9.   How do you rate the value of karmic capitalism as compared to other goals and responsibilities in your life? List your specific reasons for placing a high value on attaining financial independence.

10.   How willing are you to give this work some priority in your life? How much priority are you willing to give this project? Are you ready to commit time and energy to working with consciousness expansion techniques?

11.   Summarize your beliefs about good and evil when considering abundance. Is there anything about attaining financial independence that you consider evil? If so, elaborate. How might your beliefs about good and evil affect your work with karmic capitalism?

12.   How do you feel about your power to create your reality? In what areas of your life do you feel powerless? To what degree do you feel you own your power and can use it to bring what you want into your life?

13.   Write down any other limiting beliefs or issues that come to mind when thinking about attaining abundance.

For each of your answers to the above questions:

1.   Prepare a concise one or two sentence statement reflecting your beliefs.

2.   Place any belief you consider limiting on a separate page.

3.   Prepare a new positive belief to replace the limiting ones. This new belief could be the complete opposite of your previous belief.

4.   Again prepare a concise one or two sentence affirmation describing this new positive belief. Use the present tense as if the new belief were already true.

5.   Use the superconscious mind script and repeat your affirmations to yourself. Do this with conviction, and act as if each and every one of these statements were true today.

When you formulate affirmations and visualizations to alter previous beliefs choose new beliefs that will correspond to what you want to achieve. For limiting beliefs begin by focusing on a new belief that is opposite of the old one. For those beliefs that represent too low a goal, simply adjust them to test your karmic capitalistic muscle.

The exercises I will present in the next chapter are an ideal opportunity to test your ability to reprogram your subconscious with new expansive and positive beliefs. Always select a belief that represents the next stage in your growth process in that area. By "raising the bar" you promote advancing to the next level of karmic capitalistic training. If you are bored, the belief was too small a stretch. Frustration usually indicates the belief was too great a step at this time.

Look for reasons why your previous beliefs were limiting and see the mistakes you were making in your thinking when altering your beliefs. This functions to sharpen your ability to prepare and follow far more functional beliefs that will lead to abundance. Any difficulties you encounter with this system will be equal to what you expected. To master this system expect no difficulty and assume complete success.

In order to facilitate your entrance into the realm of karmic capitalism, you must feel safe with this approach. You absolutely have the power to create a personally safe reality through accessing your Higher Self. You can tune in to a mental climate that will promote the growth of your being. Any fears otherwise generated simply function to create anxiety, drain your creative energy and reduce your motivation to continue with this program.

Designing and using an affirmation belief exercise to this effect will help you in your capitalistic endeavors. A sample affirmation in this area would be: "I create my reality of abundance and financial independence."

You are now making quite a different use of your consciousness than in the past. Persistence is required, and your desire can be amplified through the proper use of affirmations and visualizations. The results you attain will be directly proportional to the intensity of your commitment and desire. Saying to yourself daily, "I'm really excited about karmic capitalism. I am 100 percent committed to working with these techniques and I practice every day" is an example of what I am talking about.

When I was a teenager during the 1960s, the predominant belief about capitalism was that if you were over 30 and affluent you must be evil. I never did accept this ridiculous belief, and subsequently alienated several of my classmates in college. The impressionability of so many people is more than unfortunate. As a budding karmic capitalist, I maintained my open and expansive positive belief system. Like all aspects of the universe, the over 30-affluent "evil" paradigm passed into history. There is nothing wrong with being over 30 and successful.

It is extremely important to realize that what you are is fundamentally good; so are other people and the universe in which we function. This attitude will lead to your treating yourself and others with love and respect, and will act to facilitate both your spiritual growth and the attainment of financial independence. It will also promote the acceptance of the fact that there is nothing to fear about attaining your financial goals.

Applying the principles from these exercises will have the positive effect of utilizing the power of your thoughts and imagination to achieve success in the specific areas of attracting abundance and spiritual growth. Belief that you indeed possess this power will enable you to more fully harness it.

AN EXERCISE TO FORMULATE AND INCORPORATE AFFIRMATIONS

Use the previous exercises to formulate new and healthy beliefs. Begin to formulate new beliefs to replace the old ones. Prepare simple statements to represent these positive beliefs on the same sheet of paper. Your new affirmation is a new expression of your evolving consciousness.

After you have decided on the wording of your belief affirmation, write out the final wording using the present tense. Now create a mental image of this affirmation. This visualization should represent the substance of your belief. Many prefer to create mental movies, during which your abundance goals unfold. Crystallize your visualization into a clear, powerful image of what your desires are.

To make your visualizations more effective, incorporate these simple suggestions:
- Create a single image representative of your goal.
- Place yourself in this image exactly as you would like yourself to be.
- Incorporate emotions into this image.
- Your mental movie may be symbolic or literal – just make sure it's meaningful to you.
- Place any environmental or other component in it that is pleasing and works in conjunction with the purpose of this image.

For example, you can use the image of yourself as a self-employed and very successful entrepreneur, who is spiritually empowered and fulfilled in all aspects of life. You could also use the image of an eagle soaring over the mountains instead. In this imagery the mountains represent potential obstacles to your financial and spiritual goals that are no longer a serious impediment to you.

You do not have to use visualizations with each component of these exercises. Affirmations by themselves are acceptable, but the combination of visualizations, or mental movies, and affirmations is far better. Adjust these techniques as you progress both in these exercises and in your spiritual unfoldment.

Write your visualization for the first topic you practice with below the corresponding affirmation. Continue with this procedure for each subject area you decided to work on until you have a final affirmation and visualization for each. When you have finished, take a new sheet of paper and put the heading "Karmic Capitalism Affirmations and Visualizations" at the top. On this sheet, write out the final versions of all the affirmations and corresponding visualizations you have been working on, skipping a couple of lines between each. Use this sheet in the next exercises.

This next exercise is a simple method for using affirmations and visualizations to effectively alter your belief systems. If you truly allow yourself to accept the belief that you can attain karmic capitalism, then that is the reality you will create. Each individual can choose to focus on and accept whatever beliefs he or she wants.

These exercises are designed to train you in the art of altering your beliefs. Just because in the past you have adopted limiting and self-defeating beliefs, it doesn't mean you can't change them at any time. It is only through deliberate and stubborn resistance that you will allow the previously accepted beliefs to continue to be a part of your reality.

Accept the fact that you can accomplish these time-tested techniques. Formulating excuses for not practicing these exercises is part of the old you, and not at all characteristic of a karmic capitalist. A new future of abundance awaits you as you put your faith in this system, even before you have physical evidence to support it.

You will be far better off if you put aside your doubts for now, and proceed to program yourself to a frame of mind that will be conducive to what you want to achieve. You don't have to completely obliterate your doubts—just put them on the back burner for awhile.

Affirmation/visualization exercises are simple and fun to practice. You need only apply them to the new beliefs you have developed for this specific topic. Here is an example of a simple affirmation/visualization exercise.

It is best to develop a habit of practicing this exercise at the same time each day. To thoroughly benefit from this approach, I strongly recommend you practice first with the superconscious mind technique. Now breathe deeply and systematically relax your body by any method you feel comfortable. Clear your mind of all thoughts and worries. A simple recommendation is to listen to some relaxing New Age music for a few minutes as you clear your mind.

Now use the sheet of paper containing the final versions of your affirmations and visualizations. Start with your first affirmation and begin to speak it, either aloud or in your mind. Say it with a deliberate and confident forcefulness. Believe what you are saying as you say it. During the exercise you are to "pretend" that what you are saying is already true. Keep your focus of attention exclusively on the topic at hand. Repeat the statement over and over, and then begin using your visualization. Imagine it as vividly as you can. If you are visualizing some thing or situation that you want, imagine that you have already achieved your goal.

Allow your imagination free reign during this procedure. With each visualization, see the event leading to abundance actually occurring. Feel the exhilaration and excitement accompanying your success. As an illustration, suppose you are working on changing your beliefs about your ability to make good business decisions. Perceive yourself making a specific business decision and follow it through to illustrate that this was an ethical win-win-win approach that resulted in you benefiting significantly financially, while growing spiritually at the same time. Create a feeling of pride and fulfillment to accompany this visualization.

When you have completed your first exercise, proceed with the second, then the third, and so on until you are finished. Some of these topics require only a minute or two on each one. Others may take between five and fifteen minutes for a specific area. Anything over fifteen minutes in one area is unnecessary. Experience will allow you to develop a practical regimen.

Never underestimate the potential of this technique due to its simplicity. You are unleashing an ability of spirituality that can be used to literally change the course of your life. You've got nothing to lose by giving it a try. It is applicable for conscious creation in any area. When relaxing to do your exercises, realize that spending a few minutes imagining something accomplishes work. When you direct the power of your imagination, you are harnessing the creative forces of nature and putting them to work for you. This is what a karmic capitalist does on a daily basis.

Regular application of the exercises presented in this book is necessary to make the changes in beliefs you so desire. Get into a pattern of daily practice for several weeks. Don't miss a day. Later on, if you skip a day or two, it won't matter. Remember to feel free to update and change your exercises whenever you have reached a goal or simply feel like adjusting them.

A further application of your training will be evident in the early stages of your practice sessions. Your defense mechanisms will attempt to distract you from your goals. These methods allow you to examine your beliefs about these attempts to sabotage your efforts and to reshape your ideas as needed.

ABUNDANCE VISUALIZATION EXERCISE

Practice the superconscious mind technique and then focus on the following abundance goals:
1.   I will have a minimum annual income or net worth of $_____ in exactly 6 months.
2.   My annual income or net worth in 12 months will be $_____.
3.   In five years my annual income or net worth will be
$_____.
4.   My life in the future will be characterized by attracting fellow karmic capitalists, just like me. I now see myself in exactly one year doing just what I want to do, attaining abundance and being surrounded by like-minded souls.
5.   Repeat the above goal for three years, five years, ten years and so on.

This exercise will assist you in removing limiting beliefs about abundance, and focus your subconscious on your vision of becoming a karmic capitalist. You must recognize the fact that committing yourself to abundance goals means investing a certain amount of your energy in income-producing functions.

Devising a game plan with specific goals is necessary for success in this endeavor. Stating simply to yourself "I want to be rich" or "I will earn more money" is inadequate to realize these objectives. You must be specific. Attracting fellow karmic capitalists is important, since some of them may serve as examples, offer constructive advice or become business partners with you in future business enterprises.

USING YOUR DREAMS TO CHANGE BELIEFS

Now that you have been able to experiment with affirmations and visualization exercises, you are ready to apply these methods to your dream state. I have previously described a simple dream programming exercise in chapter 2.

Initiate a pattern of remembering, recording, and interpreting your dreams. Then experiment a little with controlling your dreams. This prepares you for lucid dreaming [dreaming in which you realize you are in a dream]. Recording your dreams is a method of placing a value on them, and a part of your consciousness that is representative of your spirituality. This change in attitude and behavior automatically sets in motion wheels that will lead to greater communication between your subconscious and Higher Self.

We all dream every night for three hours. It is usually a simple matter to remember dreams by using suggestion.

Prior to sleep, simply repeat any of the following suggestions several times in your mind:

•   I am going to remember my dreams.

•   I am going to remember my dreams and write them down immediately upon awakening.

•   I am going to wake up right after a dream and remember it thoroughly.

•   I am going to wake up right after the most important dream [dreams] of the evening and remember it fully.

•   My subconscious is being programmed to allow me to recall every dream important to my spiritual growth.

Recording your dreams gives them permanence. The simplest method is to use a tape recorder, followed by a summary of these nightly movies in a journal. Here are some helpful hints to assist you in your dream journaling:

•   Keep your notebook or recorder within reach of where you are sleeping.

•   Upon awakening from a dream, don't get out of bed. Reach for your notebook or recorder, and record the dream immediately.

•   Record the dream in as much detail as possible, including any emotions you experienced at any point in the dream.

•   Record any interpretations, insights or associations as you jot down your dream.

•   Be aware that initially only a few scraps of your dream may be recalled. Continue recording anything you can remember, no matter how irrelevant it may seem. Once you get the flow of information moving, more data will follow.

You can tape-record your dreams at least four times faster than you can write them down. Eventually you have to write them

down later. It is advisable to do so immediately.

To use your dreams specifically for abundance requires a simple preprogramming. The first step is to design the content of your dream to fulfill some aspect of karmic capitalism. Some sample preprogramming suggestions to say to yourself just prior to falling asleep are:

- Tonight I am going to have a dream that will give me insight about any obstacles to attaining abundance.
- Tonight I am going to have a dream that will help me to sharpen my business skills and eliminate any beliefs that have inhibited these abilities in the past.
- Tonight I am going to have a dream that will give me insight about how I can improve my spirituality.
- Tonight I am going to have a dream that will help me to get back in touch with my Higher Self.
- Tonight I am going to have a dream showing me a successful karmic capitalist.

Simply give yourself the suggestion just prior to sleep. It's best to give yourself suggestions after your mind has quieted down and you are extremely relaxed. You can also use visualization to program your desired dream. Simply imagine the dream happening just the way you want it to happen. Visualize it in your mind as vividly as you can, repeat your suggestions to yourself for a minute or so, and let yourself drop off to sleep.

We are dealing with nonphysical reality in the dream technique, so a few statements about your beliefs concerning this world is appropriate at this time. If you have a strong orientation toward believing that the physical world is the only one that should be taken seriously or thought of as "real," this belief will color your experience in a lucid dream. Nonphysical reality is extremely responsive to thought. Keep an open mind to prevent interfering with the flow of energy from both the subconscious and Higher Self, which are continually active in dreamworld. This situation can be easily handled by adding this belief to the list you worked on in the previous sections.

Here is a simple visualization exercise you can practice to begin changing your beliefs. This technique may also be used just prior to retiring at night to preprogram your dream state.

In this exercise all obstacles to karmic capitalism will be removed.

1. Get comfortable, close your eyes and relax yourself using any method you prefer. Try the progressive relaxation approach I previously described.

2. Imagine yourself opening up a door and seeing yourself asleep in your bed with several blankets covering your body. Each of these blankets represents an obstacle to attaining financial independence.

3.   Mentally label each of these blankets with a large white sticker that represents this particular impediment. As you remove each blanket, you are effectively eliminating this obstacle from your path toward karmic capitalism.

4.   Visualize yourself reading the label on the outermost blanket. It says procrastination. Remove this blanket and feel procrastination being eliminated from your awareness.

5.   Now look at the next blanket, which contains a label that reads low self-image. Remove this blanket and feel this low self-image being eliminated from your awareness.

6.   The next blanket says poor organization. Remove this blanket and feel poor organization being eliminated from your awareness.

7.   Poor concentration is seen on the label of the next blanket. Remove this blanket and feel poor concentration being eliminated from your awareness.

8.   The next blanket says depression. Remove this blanket and feel depression being eliminated from your awareness.

9.   The next blanket reads cynicism. Remove this blanket and feel cynicism being eliminated from your awareness.

10.   Compulsive spending is found on the next blanket label. Remove this blanket and feel compulsive spending being eliminated from your awareness.

11.   The next blanket reads self-defeating sequences. Remove this blanket and feel any remaining self-defeating sequences, or self-sabotage, from your awareness.

12.   Now spend a few minutes enjoying this relaxed state as you are now prepared to accept and incorporate the lifestyle of a karmic capitalist. Open your eyes and resume your normal activities when you are ready.

CHAPTER 5

PROGRAMMING THE SUBCONSCIOUS FOR ABUNDANCE

If you decide to only give power to those things, circumstances and people that support you in attaining abundance, you have successfully reprogrammed your subconscious to effect this goal. This chapter will explain exactly how this mechanism works.

Your subconscious is programmed daily by media advertisements, sales pitches and other attempts to influence your behavior. This in itself is a big business we call advertising. Politicians use these principles to get elected, and corporations apply these concepts to make money.

Throughout our life we learn to noncritically accept certain suggestions, and a status quo lifestyle is created. At other times we critically challenge any attempt to alter this programming. You can reprogram your mind at any time to accomplish anything that is humanly possible.

We are all in possession of two very distinct ways of processing information. The technical terms for these levels of consciousness are conscious mind proper (conscious mind for short) and the subconscious mind. The conscious mind is a type of censor that critically evaluates all of the hundreds of thousands of data we are exposed to daily by way of our five senses. It decides what is acceptable and what will be rejected from affecting the subconscious.

The subconscious functions as a computer and uncritically accepts whatever programming is given to it by the conscious mind or defense mechanisms (ego). The Higher Self also programs the subconscious, but normally this Higher Self, or superconscious mind, allows the conscious mind to do the programming. It is only when we specifically call upon the Higher Self (as in a superconscious mind tap) do we change the usual method of subconscious programming.

Hypnosis is a natural method of setting aside the conscious mind and presenting suggestions directly to the subconscious in order to reprogram the latter. We can also use hypnosis to access the Higher Self to effect spiritual growth via the cleansing mechanism previously described.

Unless you reprogram the subconscious, previous beliefs, behavior patterns and self-defeating sequences remain a part of your awareness. These past limitations will make it impossible to attain karmic capitalism. Any positive goals or ideas will be repelled if they are inconsistent with the programming currently within your subconscious.

Each experience we have creates a thought, which when reinforced becomes a belief. Our beliefs create both our habits and ways of responding to the world around us. A viable solution to improper beliefs rests on the fact that what you believe to be true becomes a part of your new reality. Our thoughts literally create our universe, as demonstrated by quantum physics.

To change your life you must alter your thoughts. It is your perception of the world around you that determines both your reality and your actions. We can reprogram our mind when we establish a noncritical acceptance of new ideas on a subconscious level. Hypnosis is the ideal method to accomplish this reprogramming.

When you receive information from an outside source (other people, the media, and so forth) and you accept it as truth, that's programming. Self-programming occurs when you say things to yourself. The moment you believe, and accept it as truth, you have been programmed. Conversely, anytime you communicate information to another person that they accept to be true you have programmed them. The easiest way to initiate this self-programming is through the use of self-hypnosis tapes.

As we discuss the functioning of the subconscious mind, there are certain principles of mind-body medicine you should be aware of. Here are some key concepts in this paradigm:

1.   The subconscious will be easier to program the more we can distract the conscious mind. This implies a setting aside of the conscious mind so that we may communicate directly with the subconscious. Hypnosis does just that. Trying to force yourself to make changes by attempts at will power (conscious mind) alone fail miserably. Examples of this are trying to eliminate a habit, or to will yourself to sleep during a restless evening.

Suggestions about who you are bring about more rapid changes in behavior and attitude than those concerning what you do. For example, "I am a financially independent karmic capitalist" is more effective than saying "I have the ability to earn a great deal of money."

2.   The body responds to the subconscious mind's programming. We can trace the cause of any physical problem to the mind. Any emotional

response has as its predecessor a thought that conditioned the subconscious to respond in a certain way. We can use this system to properly reprogram the subconscious to no longer interpret certain situations in your life with anxiety and thus build up our resistance to life's potential stresses.

3.   Your expectations creates situations that manifest these thoughts. When we focus on a dominant thought, the universe cooperates by making that possibility a reality. If you are worried about running into a supervisor at work because you came in late, for example, don't be surprised if you see him or her at the water cooler.

4.   It is easier to add more complex programming to the subconscious once simpler suggestions have already been accepted. This is the basis of hypnotherapy. We use relaxation suggestions to both distract the conscious mind, and allow comfortable feelings to spread throughout the body. Once this has been accomplished it is easier to present to the subconscious, and have accepted, more difficult suggestions. Nothing succeeds like success. This relates to the ancient Hermetic philosophy that "like attracts like."

5.   We tend to find what we are looking for. The subconscious always moves in the direction of our dominant thoughts. It responds faster to suggestions that reflect previous programming or benefits. If you are looking for good in a person or situation, that is what you focus on and will ultimately find. The reverse also applies. Karmic capitalists always focus on positivity.

6.   The subconscious mind's programming stays the same unless it is replaced by a different program. Time may heal a physical injury, but it will not bring about a change in what your subconscious has previously accepted. You must take direct action to replace improper beliefs with new ones. Self-hypnosis is the most efficient and effective way to accomplish this.

7.   Our imagination can bring about more quality changes in our universe than any amount of data. We operate on what we believe to be true. Living your life as if you are a karmic capitalist now will speed up the process of making this goal a reality, even if you possess none of the characteristics I described in chapter 1 at this time.

8.   The subconscious tends to move toward pleasure and away from pain. I am not advocating aversive conditioning, but structuring your new programming to present the lifestyle of a karmic capitalist as attractive as possible to the subconscious. This way the subconscious will assist you in your goal, since it naturally is attracted to suggestions it considers pleasurable.

You can now begin to understand how the subconscious mind works, and how we can reprogram it to attain desired goals.

POSITIVE THINKING ALONE VERSUS
HYPNOTIC PROGRAMMING

There are plenty of books written on the power of positive thinking. Using positive thinking alone without reprogramming the subconscious is bound to result in failure eventually. The conscious mind, or will power, is the agent involved in positive thinking, and this component of our mind resists change. Will power is only temporary, as anyone we who has tried to overcome a habit will verify.

We must move beyond positive thinking alone and permanently change our beliefs. This can only be done by reprogramming the subconscious. This is the reason self-hypnosis is so successful when used properly. Your subconscious is responsible for creating your reality, not the ego.

By further enlisting the aid of the Higher Self through cleansing techniques, you raise your self-image permanently, and this new you now contains a set of beliefs that fosters karmic capitalism. You are never too young or old to initiate this process of becoming a karmic capitalist.

A technique I developed several years ago that I refer to as spiritual restructuring will enable you to apply self-hypnosis exercises to establishing yourself as a karmic capitalist.

Here is a sample exercise that is easy to practice and incorporates the basis of this spiritual restructuring.

1.   Prepare a list of beliefs and/or behavioral patterns that you would like to change or remove from you awareness. Always maintain a positive approach, so that you list these items in terms of what you would like, rather than what you don't want. An example would be "I am becoming more motivated and organized" is much preferable to "I don't procrastinate and fall behind on my wok."

2.   Add to your list the situations or times of the day when dysfunctional behaviors or beliefs were exhibited.

3.   Now list the advantages of making permanent changes by eliminating these previous beliefs or behaviors.

4.   Access your Higher Self by practicing the superconscious mind tap exercise I presented in chapter 2. During one of the open spaces in the script ask your Higher Self to show you specifically how to permanently alter these beliefs, or eliminate the negative behaviors. Reinforce your ability to successfully apply this method by saying to yourself "I am ready, willing and able to initiate cleansing."

5.   While still in trance, direct your focus on the future. Ask your Higher Self to guide you to a future date during which your goals are accomplished. Perceive yourself functioning as a karmic capitalist at this time.

6.   Stay in this trance for as long as you like and open your eyes to resume normal conscious mind functioning.

Throughout my career as a hypnotherapist I have emphasized two main paradigms. The first one is that we tend to initiate a form of self-sabotage that I call "self-defeating sequences" whenever a desirable situation presents itself, and our self-image is too low. Secondly, psychic empowerment is the most important lesson our soul needs to learn during its sojourn on the physical plane. Fear is the main antagonist to psychic empowerment and spiritual growth.

If you don't attain abundance, or any other goal, it is because you didn't feel worthy of this goal, or you feared it. Spiritual principles teach us that we cannot make permanent changes in our behavior and thought processes until we have actually become the person we want to be.

Consider the goal to become financially independent. Now add to this a problem with compulsive spending. Unless you become the person who has overcome compulsive spending, you will never permanently establish yourself as a financially independent karmic capitalist. You may earn significant amounts of money, but you will spend more than you earn, and have to earn it all over again. You simply can't win that way.

In the example I just presented, it would be impossible to classify you as a karmic capitalist. Karmic capitalism implies a high degree of spiritual growth. Spiritually evolved souls simply don't have issues of compulsive spending.

Here is a simple exercise to assist you in visualizing yourself as you would like to become. Practice any form of relaxation prior to using this script:

Mentally see an image of yourself standing before you. This is your body exactly as you would like it to appear, exactly as you want that body to be and as it has the possibility of being. Look at it more and more closely now, and it will be a realistic but ideal body image, one that you really could achieve, and one that you will achieve. And when you have a very clear image of your body as you would like to have it, keep observing that image, and make it a part of your own reality.

PLAY NEW AGE MUSIC FOR 4 MINUTES

That ideal body image is becoming more and more real, you are seeing it very clearly, and seeing it in its full size and dimensions, and now you are going to step forward and into that body, you will find yourself in that body, so that you can try it out and make certain that it is just the body you do want to have, and if there is something you would like to change, then make those changes now.

Move around in that body, feel its strength and agility, its dynamic aliveness, its surging vitality, and make really certain that its appearance and all of its attributes are what you realistically desire. And, as you occupy that body, coming to know that body very well, your present physical body is going to be drawn into that new mold. You are moving already toward the realization of that ideal body image, and you will be doing whatever is needed to achieve that body you want to have.

PLAY NEW AGE MUSIC FOR 5 MINUTES
END TRANCE AS USUAL

The principles and practices of karmic capitalism demonstrate that when you are putting out supportive, loving energy into your universe you will surround yourself with supportive, loving individuals. The more you raise your own soul's growth, the more joy and fulfillment you will experience. We tend to notice what we expect and meet up with people and circumstances that are representative of the energy we send out to the universe.

It is our thoughts that begin this process. When you think about becoming a karmic capitalist, spiritually evolved methods of attaining abundance in a win-win-win approach surface and direct your attention.

Always be yourself. The ancients said "Know thyself." Do not simply pick a mentor and model yourself after him or her. There is no empowerment in that approach. Besides, what worked for them may not be successful for you. Analyze and alter your present beliefs, rather than conforming and trying to mold yourself into someone you are not.

Business relationships are reflections of our inner awareness and level of spiritual growth. All relationships exhibit the "mirror of karma." By becoming exactly who you want to be as a spiritually evolved karmic capitalist, you will attract like-minded souls into your life at all levels.

Repeated difficulties in business and with certain key people in the workplace requires an examination of yourself. Look within your own mirror of karma and objectively note the types of characteristics you possess that may be sending out this negative form of energy.

Your next step is to work on these traits and become the person you want to attract. When you establish yourself as a karmic capitalist, with all of the ethical, spiritual and abundance characteristics, your world will mirror this growth by providing you with business situations and people that manifest this new you.

Another important consideration in reprogramming the subconscious with karmic capitalism as your goal is to eliminate neediness. A karmic capitalist may want some goal, but he or she is never needy. Nobody wants to be around a needy individual. This person is simply expressing their insecurities and helplessness.

Reprogramming involves changing previous dysfunctional or inaccurate beliefs to more productive ones. You must commit yourself to this quest. The degree of abundance you attain is

directly proportional to your level of commitment.

In addition, a specific date should be decided on to begin this process. There is no better time than the present. Have specific goals in mind. You may desire a specific promotion or new job. A certain income level or net worth value may be stated to your subconscious. The main point here is to be specific. It does your karmic capitalistic goals no good to simply say "I want to have a lot of money."

When you initiate this process it is critical to use repetitive action. One example of this principle is to play your self-hypnosis tape daily. Acting as if your goals are already established even though this may feel awkward at first, is another example.

There are times when you will become distracted and veer off your game plan. It is important to place yourself back on track as soon as possible. My tapes are especially designed to speed up this process.

Another way to accomplish this is through self-talk. This approach allows you to forgive yourself and continue on with your program. A good example of self-talk is the dialogue you can have with yourself following a procrastination incident, during which you lost a sale. Simply say to yourself "I am aware of this slip in my new programming, and will not let this error be repeated. I am a confident, motivated karmic capitalist who will attain abundance."

We must overcome procrastination to become a karmic capitalist. Since persistence is the opposite of procrastination, here are some behaviors you can adopt that will facilitate persistence:

• Be thoroughly organized.
• Have a definite purpose and an established game plan as part of your planning.
• Maintain a high level of cooperation with others in reference to your quest.

- Use your own ingenuity and self-reliance (empowerment) skills daily on everything you do.
- Establish a solid factual foundation by doing your homework.
- Develop an intense desire for your goals.

The self-hypnosis script I am about to present may be used with any of the scripts presented in this book. You can also use the superconscious mind tap script presented in chapter 2 prior to practicing with these exercises. The following is a standard progressive relaxation self-hypnosis exercise:

Begin with the forehead. Loosen the muscles in your forehead. Now your eyes. Loosen the muscles around your eyes. Your eyelids relax. Now your face, your face relaxes. And your mouth...relax the muscles around your mouth, and even the inside of your mouth. Your chin; let it sag and feel heavy. And as you relax your muscles, your breathing continues r-e-g-u-l-a-r-l-y and d-e-e-p-l-y, deeply within yourself. Now your neck, your neck relaxes. Every muscle, every fiber in your neck relaxes. Your shoulders relax,...your arms...your elbows...your forearms...your wrists...your hands...and your fingers relax. Your arms feel loose and limp; heavy and loose and limp. Your whole body begins to feel loose and limp. Your neck muscles relax; the front of your neck; the back muscles. Keep breathing deeply and relax. Now your chest. The front part of your chest relaxes and the back part of your chest relaxes. Your abdomen...the pit of your stomach, that relaxes. The small of your back, loosen the muscles. Your hips...your thighs...your knees relax...even the muscles in your legs. Your ankles...your feet...and your toes. Your whole body feels loose and limp. And now as you feel the muscles relaxing, you will notice that you begin to feel heavy and relaxed and tired all over. Your body begins to feel v-e-r-y, v-e-r-y tired and you are going to feel d-r-o-w-s-i-e-r and d-r-o-w-s-i-e-r, from the top of your head right down to your toes. Every breath you take is going to deepen this trance. Deeper and deeper and deeper relaxed. You feel your body getting drowsier and drowsier.

Alright now. Sleep now and rest. You did very well. Listen very carefully. I'm going to count forwards now from 1-5. When I reach the count of 5 you will be able to remember everything you experienced and re-experienced you'll feel very relaxed refreshed, you'll be able to do whatever you have to planned for the rest of the day or evening. You'll feel very positive about what you've just experienced and very motivated about your confidence and ability to play this tape again to experience self-hypnosis. Alright now. 1 very very deep, 2 you're getting a little bit lighter, 3 you're getting much much lighter, 4 very very light, 5 awaken. Wide awake and refreshed.

THE LIMITS OF HYPNOSIS

There quite simply are no limits to what self-hypnosis can accomplish. As long as your goal is humanly possible, you are truly motivated to attain it, you have faith in your ability to be successful, you have the discipline to practice simple exercises and you somehow access your Higher Self, you cannot fail.

In Soul Healing I describe how my patients have used the superconscious mind tap to shrink cancer tumors and build up their immune system to fight AIDS. Another dramatic example of the power we all have with self-hypnosis is firewalking demonstrations.

Many thousands of Americans and Europeans since the early 1980s have successfully walked across beds of burning coals without damaging their feet.

The smooth bed of burning coals are heated to a temperature of from 1200 to 1400 degrees Fahrenheit. This is more than hot enough to inflict serious burns to the soles of the feet. Skeptics are quick to come up with impotent theories such as a protective layer of perspiration is formed on the soles of the feet ("Leidenfrost effect"), or an insulating layer of coal ash protects the feet from burning.

Whatever the real mechanism is, it is dramatic. Any skeptic is welcome to try firewalking without the appropriate belief system. I highly suggest they book a room at their local hospital and be prepared for the most excruciating pain they ever felt if they do. The fact is that the adoption of the belief that their feet will be unharmed results in just that after walking across these hot coals.

The "placebo effect" in drug research is also based on the subject's beliefs. If they accept a suggestion that a sugar pill (an inert substance or control) is a miracle drug, the healing that results is entirely due to the powers of the subconscious.

Many years ago a researcher named Dr. Philip West reported a man he treated suffering from advance stages of cancer with an experimental drug called Krebiozen. The patient desperately wanted this drug to work, and after just one dose his tumor masses shrunk considerably.

Later, this patient read reports describing how ineffective Krebiozen was following several clinical tests. His cancer began to spread. Dr. West now lied to him and informed this patient of a new more potent Krebiozen that the doctor now gave him.

The patient was given plain water, but his condition markedly improved. Shortly thereafter this same patient read reports that the American Medical

Association and the Food and Drug Administration has conclusively proved the worthlessness of Krebiozen. He again suffered from the spread of his cancer tumors and soon died.

These examples are meant to illustrate the time tested principle that our experience of reality is strongly affected by our experiencing what we perceive as reality—which most of the time reinforces the beliefs.

With this in mind, practice these self-hypnosis exercises with an expectation of success. You may obtain professionally recorded tapes with my voice either through Llewellyn or my office of each of the scripts presented.

OVERCOMING PROCRASTINATION

Now that you have mastered the simple art of self-hypnosis, try this script on overcoming procrastination:

You are persistent, determined and ambitious. You complete each task because you are a success-oriented winner. You fulfill each personal and professional desire in a relentless, yet efficient and empowered way. You have the self-discipline to accomplish all of your personal and professional goals. Each day that passes will result in an increase in your self-discipline. You can now complete large and complicated tasks by breaking them down into smaller components and doing each job one step at a time. You are clear and focused on your values and have no reservations about committing to your goals. You remain alert and focused upon what you are doing. You can routinely block out all thoughts except those related to what you are doing. You are a winner and will now always exhibit a success-type personality. You are self-reliant and self-confident. You are filled with independence and determination. At all times you function like a karmic capitalist. You project a very positive self-image and can do whatever you set your mind to. You evaluate the various factors of a goal objectively and decide what you want quickly. You have the courage and inner strength to make life-changing decisions and carry them out. You do what you say you'll do. You finish what you start. You fulfill your commitments. You do it today not tomorrow. You have the power and ability to do more in less time. You use a schedule and make it work for you. You increase your speed and productivity. You finish your projects. You have the power and ability to create any reality you desire.

ELIMINATE GUILT AND WORRY

Eliminating feelings of guilt over past actions and worry concerning the future is necessary to attaining abundance through karmic capitalism approaches. Try this script to achieve this goal:

You are at peace with yourself and your past. You forgive yourself. You learn from the past and you release it. Every day, you feel better and better, all over, in every way. You are positive and your life becomes positive. You now see problems only as opportunities. You become positive and optimistic. You now develop clarity about your desires and goals. You evaluate the potentials and decide what you want. You now have the courage to make life-changing decisions. You now let go of all fears. You are self-assured and confident about your future. You draw joyous experiences into your life. You create a positive new life. You create your own reality, and you create a beautiful life. You release yourself. You are free. You are confident and secure. You retain a calm, optimistic outlook. You feel powerful and in control. Your mind is calm and you think positive thoughts. You now accept the things you cannot change, and change the things you can. You create a happy, successful new reality. You are self-confident and self-reliant. You are worthy and deserving. You let go of the past, are responsible to the present, and create a positive new future.

You release your fears, and manifest your desires. You deserve love, prosperity and happiness. You mentally, emotionally and spiritually detach from all forms of negativity and negative people. From this moment on you will project a positive, loving, self-confident and empowered self-image that will permanently eliminate any previous guilt and worry from your awareness.

Mentally see yourself incorporating these suggestions into your new reality and functioning as a karmic capitalist.

PLAY NEW AGE MUSIC FOR 3 MINUTES

1.   Visualize yourself in your favorite relaxing environment. This may be the beach, a park or a cabin in the woods. Add to this sounds of nature and the time of the year that you enjoy most.

2.   Imagine yourself walking along in your favorite environment while looking up at the sky. You notice a rainbow has appeared and you focus your attention on the colors. You see red, yellow, blue, green, orange, purple and violet.

3.   As you stare at this rainbow, you realize that as long as you can see it you can accomplish anything you want to do. It is not necessary for this

rainbow to be present for you to accomplish your goal, but its presence assures a successful attainment of any quest.

4.   Sit down now and think of the kind of person you would like to become, a person completely free from guilt and worry. Review personality traits, health issues, finances, and relationships. Focus on specific goals and aspects of your personality. Look up again and note the rainbow. You are now able to accomplish this goal of becoming who you want to be. All of your guilt and worries have now disappeared. Do this now.

PLAY NEW AGE MUSIC FOR 4 MINUTES

POSITIVE THINKING AND ACTIONS

This next script deals with reprogramming your subconscious for positive thinking and actions:

Every day...your mind will become much calmer and clearer...more composed...more placid...more tranquil. You will become much less easily worried...much less easily agitated...much less fearful and apprehensive...much less easily upset.

Every day...you will feel a greater feeling of personal well-being...a greater feeling of personal safety and security...than you have felt for a long, long time. Every day...you will become...and you will remain...more and more completely relaxed...both mentally and physically.

And as you become...and as you remain...more relaxed...and less tense each day...so you will develop much more confidence in yourself...Much more confidence in your ability to do...not only what you have to do each day...but also...much more confidence in your ability to do whatever you ought to be able to do...without fear of failure...without fear of consequences...without anxiety...without uneasiness. Because of this...every day...you will feel more and more independent...more able to "stick up for yourself"...to stand upon your own two feet...to hold your own no matter how difficult or trying things may be.

Every day, in every way, you are getting better, better and better...Negative thoughts and negative suggestions have no influence over you at any mind level.

You see positive opportunities in everything you experience. Every day, you feel better about yourself. You are optimistic. You are enthusiastic and look forward to challenges. You experience the job and detach from negativity. Your positive self-image generates success and happiness. You are now at peace with yourself, the world, and everyone in it. You deserve the very best life has to offer.   You detach from pressure sand retreat to a calm inner space. You handle your responsibilities with harmonious ease. You accept the things you cannot change, and change the things you can. You are at peace with yourself and the world. You have the self-discipline to accomplish your personal and professional goals. Every day in every way, you increase your self-discipline. You do what you need to do and stop doing what doesn't work. You now adapt and you keep pace with the movements of change. You always consider your options and you always act in your best behalf. You are self-reliant and self-confident. You are filled with independence and determination. You project a very positive self-image. You can do whatever you set your mind to.

Now take a few moments and visualize yourself incorporating these suggestions.

PLAY NEW AGE MUSIC FOR 3 MINUTES

Mentally tell yourself that you are going to:

- Develop an intense desire for your goals.
- Establish a solid factual foundation by doing your homework.
- Maintain a high level of cooperation with others in reference to your quest.
- Use your own ingenuity and self-reliance (empowerment) skills daily on everything you do.
- Be thoroughly organized.
- Have a definite purpose and an established game plan as part of your own reality.
- Practice saying "Stop" every time a negative thought or self put-down enters your mind.
- Program yourself to accept compliments and loving gestures from others. Eliminate the skeptical, "What's he/she up to?" attitude.
- Tell someone you care for, "I love you." Take a risk.
- Develop a form of "positive creative aliveness." When you are in any environment, ask yourself, "How can I make this experience a memorable one?"
- Remove any illusion that your spouse, children, friends, employees and others in your life "owe" you anything simply because they live with you or work with you.
- Firmly acknowledge that you have the power to control and change your attitudes toward anything. Decide now to control your attitudes, rather than be controlled by them.

- Eliminate your tendency to analyze, assess, evaluate and interpret the world around you. Replace this counterproductive activity with being, doing and enjoying exercises.
- Reduce or eliminate the tendency to react violently or emotionally to the thoughts and behavior of others, with whom you disagree.

Say to yourself daily:

- "I don't have time for negativity."
- I set deadlines for myself and others.
- I'm continually asking myself: "What is the best use of my time right now?"
- I recognize that inevitably some of my time will be spent on activities outside my control, but I won't fret about it.
- I start with the most profitable parts of large projects and often find it is not necessary to do the rest.
- I cut off nonproductive activities as quickly as possible.
- I focus my efforts on items that will have the best long-term benefits.
- I try to enjoy whatever I am doing.
- I'm a perennial optimist.
- I build on successes.
- I handle each piece of paper only once.
- I keep my long-term goals in mind even while doing the smallest task.
- I give myself enough time to concentrate on high priority items.
- I have developed the ability to concentrate well for long stretches of time.
- I concentrate on one thing at a time.
- I delegate everything I possibly can to others.
- I make use of specialists to help me with special problems.
- I try to find a new technique each day that I can use to help gain time.
- I don't waste time regretting my failures.
- I don't waste time feeling guilty about what I don't do.
- I have confidence in my judgment of priorities and stick to them in spite of difficulties.
- I do first things first.
- I work smarter rather than harder.
- I remind myself: "There is always enough time for the important things." If it's important I'll make the time to do it.
- I keep a list of specific items to be done each day, arrange them in priority order, and then do my best to get the most important ones done as soon as possible.

- I generate as little paperwork as possible and throw away anything I possibly can.
- I am a karmic capitalist.

Now spend a few moments mentally seeing yourself, apply each and every one of these suggestions into your awareness.

PLAY NEW AGE MUSIC FOR 4 MINUTES

Another characteristic of a karmic capitalist is the ability to be decisive and make decisions quickly. He who hesitates is lost applies to the business world, as well as life in general.

In order to effectively be decisive we must use our brain more efficiently. Try this script to increase your brain power.

INCREASE YOUR BRAIN POWER

Every day you increase your ability to learn faster. As your learning ability accelerates, you remember what you learn. You easily assimilate complicated information. You think faster and more precisely. You now learn rapidly.   You are an accomplished speed reader. Your eyes vertically sweep a column of type and vertically sweep the page. There is no limit to your reading speed. You retain and recall everything. Your memory is improving. You remember everything you want to remember. You have the ability to remember everything you desire to remember. You always remember to remember. You are developing a photographic memory. You focus your concentration at will. You remain alert and focused. You block all thoughts but those related to what you are doing. Your mind has no limits. You can instantly comprehend complicated ideas. Every day, you learn faster. You remain alert and focused upon what you are doing. You are a winner. Total concentration is yours when you want it. You focus your concentration and energy at will. Every day, you increase your ability to concentrate. You can do anything you want to do.

Mentally see yourself applying each of these principles and dramatically increasing your brain power. Do this now.

PLAY NEW AGE MUSIC FOR 4 MINUTES

You can also increase your ability to engage in abstract reasoning and problem solving, mathematics, science and anything you desire to study and learn. See yourself using this improved brain power with more complicated tasks. Do this now.

PLAY NEW AGE MUSIC FOR 3 MINUTES

IMPROVING CREATIVITY

I have previously stressed the importance of creativity in the business world. Improving your creativity will do more than merely keep you ahead of the competition, it will assist you in your spiritual growth. Creativity is a right brain function that originates from our subconscious. The more you communicate directly with your Higher Self, the greater the frequency of accessing your Higher Self. One result of this mechanism is spiritual growth.

Instead of straining our defense mechanisms, or rational mind, to attempt to solve creative problems, why not allow our subconscious (accessing its Higher Self) to take on this role? Many successful creative minds (Edison, Einstein and so on) have done just that.

There are no limits to our creativity, just as no limits exist, for self-hypnosis. We can use our "right brain" for problem solving, intuitive judgment, writing, composing, inventing and other divinely inspired examples.

Here is a self-hypnosis exercise on improving creativity (an all-important skill to be mastered to assume the role of karmic capitalist). As with the other scripts, precede this with the superconscious mind exercise:

You are now going to begin the process of releasing your natural creative energy. You can unleash your creative talents by tapping into your Higher Self.

You can now draw creative inspiration from the universe. You feel creative and are creative. It is easy and natural for you to generate creative ideas and solutions.

You are open to all of the joy and fulfillment life has to offer. You an even more appreciate your natural creative expression and beauty.

The wisdom of the universe is within you. Allow your natural creative talents to flow through your awareness and manifest themselves in your present being. Do this now.

PLAY NEW AGE MUSIC FOR 4 MINUTES

Deeper and deeper in trance as you access your Higher Self and tap into your natural abilities for artistic work, for drawing, or painting, or writing or sculpting, or any kind of creative work. You easily generate creative and marketable ideas. Program your senses to facilitate bringing your ideas to an actual material form. Now let your Higher Self instruct you on your particular creative interest and mentally perceive yourself applying your creative talent in a highly developed and both personally and professionally fulfilling manner.

Focus your creative energies upon a current project, or one that you have put aside for some time. Increase your determination to its maximum level and now mentally perceive yourself carrying out this creative project successfully while enjoying this entire process. Do this now.

PLAY NEW AGE MUSIC FOR 4 MINUTES

Now for this last exercise I want you to see yourself receiving formal recognition for your creative talents. If your goal is to develop your creative talents into a full time professional pursuit, see yourself being both established, rewarded and fulfilled in this endeavor. Do this now.

PLAY NEW AGE MUSIC FOR 3 MINUTES

ASSERTIVE TRAINING

Becoming assertive is a necessary requirement for karmic capitalism. Most people are passive and allow others to manipulate them, or just sacrifice their own lives for the benefit of others. A smaller percent of the population act in an aggressive manner, during which they take advantage of others selfishly and bulldoze their way through life.

Both passive and aggressive styles are dysfunctional. Neither type facilitates growth in you or the universe. The only desirable behavior in business is an assertive approach.

Try this self-hypnosis script to develop your own assertive style of behavior:

You have certain basic rights as a soul. Among these are the following:

1.   It is your right to do anything as long as you do not purposely hurt someone else and you are willing to accept the consequences.

2.   It is your right to maintain your self-respect by answering honestly even if it does hurt someone else. This only applies to you being assertive, not aggressive.

3.   It is your right to be what you are without changing your ideas or behavior to satisfy someone else.

4.   It is your right to strive for self-fulfillment.

5.   It is your right to use your own judgement as to the need priorities of yourself and others, if you decide to accept any responsibility for another's problem.

6.   It is your right not to be subjected to negativity. It is your right to offer no excuses or justifications for your decisions or behavior.

7.   It is your right not to care.

8. It is your right to be illogical.
9. It is your right to change your mind.
10. It is your right to defend yourself without feeling self-conscious.
11. You have a right to negotiate for change.
12. You have a right to ask for help or emotional support.
13. You have a right to feel and express pain.
14. You have a right to ignore the advice of others.
15. You have a right to receive formal recognition for your work and achievements.
16. You have a right to say "no."
17. You have a right to be alone, even if others would prefer your company.
18. You have a right not to have to justify yourself to others.
19. You have a right not to take responsibility for someone else's problem.
20. You have a right not to have to anticipate other's needs and wishes.
21. You have a right not to always worry about the goodwill of others.
22. You have a right to choose not to respond to a situation.
23. You have a right to put yourself first, sometimes.
24. you have a right to make mistakes.
25. You have a right to be the final judge of your feelings and accept them as legitimate.
26. You have a right to have your own opinions and convictions.
27. You have a right to protest unfair treatment or undue criticism.
28. You have a right to interrupt in order to ask for clarification.

You are steadily increasing your ability to remove negativity from your awareness. Included among this negativity is your increasing ability to remove guilt, anger, obligation and helplessness from your awareness.

Remember, nobody has the right to take advantage of or manipulate another human being. You, and only you, are responsible for positive changes in your life and increasing your assertiveness. Once you change even one behavioral pattern you change a whole series of related behaviors. It can and will be the beginning of a whole new lifestyle.

As an assertive individual you are steadily learning to stand up for your basic rights. You are considerate of others, but you don't allow others to take advantage of you. You can act in your own best interest, and not feel guilty or wrong about it. Meekness and withdrawal, attack and blame are no longer needed with the mastery of assertive behavior. They are seen for what they are – sadly inadequate strategies of escape that create more pain and stress than they prevent. Before you can achieve assertive behavior, you must really face the fact that the passive and aggressive styles have often failed to get what you want.

The next step in assertiveness training is to develop assertive body language. Practice with the mirror will be very important as you follow these five basic rules:

1. Maintain direct eye contact.
2. Maintain an erect body posture.
3. Speak clearly, audibly and firmly.
4. Don't whine or have an apologetic tone to your voice.
5. Make use of gestures and facial expression for emphasis.

A thorough treatment of assertiveness can be found in my book Self-Hypnosis. It is only when you raise your self-image by increasing the quality of your soul's energy (cleansing) that you will achieve this assertive manner of functioning and grow spiritually at the same time.

LEADERSHIP DEVELOPMENT

A karmic capitalist is always an effective leader. This script covers a wide range of suggestions that will properly program the subconscious to facilitate your ability to take charge of business life and effectively manage others:

You become more aware daily of your inner strength. You now unleash your potential to direct and lead others. You are a powerful negotiator. You are as forceful and dynamic as you need to be. You look others straight in the eye and project a powerful image of a confident, assertive karmic capitalist.

As an effective leader, you:

- Realize that people are your most valuable asset.
- Place a priority on developing people.
- Act as a model for others to follow.
- Initiate and accept responsibility for growth.
- Develop and follow a statement of purpose.
- Make your job description and energy an integral part of the statement of purpose.
- Love people more than procedures.
- Do "win-win-win," or don't do it.
- Include others in your spiritual journey.
- Deal wisely with difficult people.
- Develop accountability for results, beginning with yourself.
- Know and do the things that give a high return.

- Communicate the strategy and vision of the organization.
- Become a change-agent and understand timing.
- Make the difficult decisions that will make a difference.
- Pour your leadership efforts into the top 20 percent of your people.
- Expose key leaders to growth opportunities.
- Are able to attract other winners/producers to the common goal.
- Surround yourself with an inner core that complements your leadership.
- Possess a genuine love for people.
- Make those who work with you more successful.
- See through other people's eyes.
- Your greatest job comes from watching others grow and develop.
- You transcend the organization.
- Identify right thinking.
- Make a public commitment to right thinking.
- Develop a plan for right thinking.

This plan includes:

- A written definition of desired right thinking.
- A way to measure progress.
- A daily measuring of progress.
- A person to whom you are accountable.
- A daily diet of self-help materials.
- Associating with right thinking people.

In addition, you are going to:

- Be responsible for who you are.
- Be responsible for what you can do.
- Be responsible for what you have received.
- Be responsible for those you lead.
- Accept accountability.

Mentally see yourself incorporating these qualities into your awareness.

PLAY NEW AGE MUSIC FOR 4 MINUTES

Other characteristics you are going to develop are:

- A positive attitude-the ability to see people and situations in a positive way.
- High energy levels-strength and stamina to work hard and not wear down.
- Personal warmth-a manner that draws people to them.

- Integrity-trustworthy, good solid character, words and walk are consistent.
- Responsibility-always "comes through," no excuses; job delegated-job done.
- Good self-image-feels good about self, others, and life.
- Mental horsepower-ability to keep learning as the job expands.
- Leadership ability-project high influence over others.
- Followership ability-willingness to submit, play team ball, and follow the leader.
- Absence of personal problems-personal, family, and business life are in order.
- People skills-the ability to draw people and develop them.
- Sense of humor-enjoys life, fails to take self too seriously.
- Resilience-able to "bounce back" when problems arise.
- Track Record-has experience and success, hopefully in two or more situations.
- Great desire-hungers for growth and personal development.
- Self-discipline-willing to "pay the price" and handle success.
- Creativity-ability to see solutions and fix problems.
- Flexibility-not afraid of change; fluid; flows as the organization grows.
- The ability to see the "big picture"-able to look beyond personal interest and see the total picture.
- Intuitive-able to discern and sense a situation without having all of the data before you.
- Empowerment

You will eliminate the following characteristics, if present, that are always associated with failed leadership.

- An over-emphasis on a title.
- Emotional instability.
- Lack of humility.
- Fear of competition from followers.
- Inability to organize details.
- Emphasis on the "authority" of leadership.
- Disloyalty.
- Expectation of pay for what they "know" instead of what they do with that which they know.
- Lack of imagination.
- Selfishness.

Visualize yourself as a leader applying each of these principles. Do that now.

PLAY NEW AGE MUSIC FOR 4 MINUTES

ATTRACTING SUCCESS

Here is a self-hypnosis exercise that truly represents the theme of this book:

Focus the power of your subconscious mind on attaining health, wealth and happiness. You are open and receptive to the good life. You know you deserve the very best that life has to offer. You can accomplish anything you set your mind to. You become more successful. There is no limit to your potential for success and excellence. You now take control of your life and create unlimited monetary abundance. Your creative thinking now opens the doors to monetary abundance. You are now totally confident of your monetary success. You now focus your energy upon making more money, and use your imagination to create more wealth. You project power and confidence at all times. You are enthusiastic and willing to act. You are persistent, ambitious and determined. You make large amounts of money. You create great wealth. What your mind can imagine, you can create. You are self-reliant, self-confident, filled with independence and determination. You have great inner courage. You project a very positive self-image. You can do whatever you set your mind to. You see positive opportunities in everything you experience. Your positive thinking creates a positive life. You are confident you can do whatever you want to do. You are optimistic and enthusiastic. You are persistent, ambitious and determined. You create the space for satisfaction and happiness in your life, and do what you need to do. You accept what you cannot change and change what you can. You now choose to view your life as happy and satisfying. You have the self-discipline to accomplish your personal and professional goals. You direct your time and energy to manifest your desires. You are clear on your values and willing to commit to your goals. You know exactly what you want and you go after it, one step at a time. You have the self-discipline to do what you need to do. You fill your life with success, happiness and peace of mind. You are willing to spend the time and energy necessary to create wealth. You take complete control of your life. You are happy and fulfilled by your independence. Success becomes your way of life. You are self-directed and free. You are a self-confident winner. You feel good about yourself. You love and believe in yourself. You do things that make you proud of yourself. Your life now becomes a series of successes. You feel an intense inner drive to accomplish your goals. You free yourself from all limitations. You project power and confidence. Your lifestyle generates high energy. Mentally perceive yourself attracting success in all facets of your personal and professional life.

PLAY NEW AGE MUSIC FOR 4 MINUTES

Now try this visualization:

Your goal is to obtain legally a certain amount of money. First, set an exact amount of money in your mind that you desire.

Now determine in your mind what service, time, effort, expertise or other aspect of your abilities you are willing to give in return for this specific sum. Set a date when you intend to receive this amount.

Next, device a game plan for your desired goal and initiate this action immediately. Write out a clear, concise statement of the amount of money you intend to acquire, name the time limit for its acquisition, state what you intend to give in return for the money, and describe clearly the plan through which you intend to accumulate it.

Now mentally incorporate the belief into your mind that you already have this amount of money. See yourself acting as if you have accomplished this goal.

PLAY NEW AGE MUSIC FOR 4 MINUTES

DREAM POWER

This script will train you to use your nightly REM cycle to facilitate your growth as a karmic capitalist:

You absolutely have the ability to use your dream levels to obtain positive and practical answers to any question you have.

You will nightly use this time to access your Higher Self to facilitate your becoming a karmic capitalist, and to access the unlimited power of your superconscious mind.

Your dreams will now be quite detailed and will impart upon you solutions to problems or goals and an increase in the quality of your soul's energy.

While in hypnosis, just before going to sleep, review a problem that can be solved with information or advice. Be sure you really care about solving it. Now say to yourself, "I want to have a dream that will contain information to solve a problem, such as _____. I will have such a dream, remember it, and understand it." Mentally see yourself doing this.

97

PLAY NEW AGE MUSIC FOR 4 MINUTES

Begin to keep a dream diary, writing down all you can remember of your dreams, and as you keep doing this you are going to discover that you can recall your dreams better and better, in more and more detail, so that your dream diary will consistently become more detailed and more accurate, and these recorded dreams are going to contribute to your development, your self-understanding.

Knowledge is power and you are now going to train your subconscious mind to release that knowledge to you so your journal and conscious memories will become filled with this knowledge and add to your power. Let your subconscious mind begin by giving you a sample of this knowledge now.

PLAY NEW AGE MUSIC FOR 4 MINUTES

AN EXERCISE TO ALTER YOUR BELIEFS CONCERNING MONEY

If you are programmed to think that money is evil, you are working against your goal of karmic capitalism. Try this exercise to develop a more positive attitude towards money:

1.   Focus in on what you don't have, while eliminating any tendency to complain about what you do possess. Every time you catch yourself falling into old and dysfunctional thought patterns, meditate on the correct viewpoint. You may focus in on such statements as, "I deserve abundance," or "My desires for prosperity are well with my karmic rights."

2.   Use self-hypnosis to ask your Higher Self for specific suggestions concerning money. Mentally perceive yourself writing down any counterproductive tendency and erasing it. Another technique is to visualize cards with these blocks written out attached to balloons and the helium filled balloons lifting these cards up in the air and permanently out of sight.

3.   Visualize your subconscious projecting your abundance goals out as positive psychic energy. Mentally see this energy connecting with mechanisms that will transform these goals into a reality.

4.   You must first have a money goal. Write it down. Keep it in your mind. Remember, everything in the material world begins on another plane. Use the mental plane to assist your subconscious in formulating the necessary psychic energy and correctly projecting it to create this reality.

5.   Always thank your Higher Self for its efforts and assistance. Be thankful and not demanding or condescending when dealing with your Higher Self.

Here is an exercise to overcome any previous obstacles you may have had to becoming a karmic capitalist:

After relaxing yourself with any technique you like, meditate on each of these questions and allow your Higher Self to assist you in the answers:

1. What circumstances have interfered with your desires for abundance?

2. Are any of these situations self-imposed? If they are self-imposed, how can you eliminate the obstacles they present?

3. Which of these are you now motivated to improve upon? Design a plan to do so.

4. What kind of balance is needed to deal constructively with each obstacle?

5. How can you achieve this balance?

6. What unnecessary obligations do you have in your life at this time?

7. How are you going to correct these?

8. When will you start this?

9. How will you begin?

10. What new goals can you work on once these obstacles are removed?

11. Where will your life be in six months? One year? Five years?

ESTABLISH YOUR KARMIC PURPOSE

This script trains you to find out what your karmic purpose is. I cannot overemphasize the importance of this information to a karmic capitalist.

Now listen very carefully. I want you to imagine a bright white light coming down from above and entering the top of your head. Filling your entire body. See it, feel it and it becomes reality. Now imagine an aura of pure white light emanating from your heart region. Again surrounding your entire body. Protecting you. See it, feel it and it becomes reality. Now only your masters and guides and highly evolved loving entities who mean you well will be able to influence you during this or any other hypnotic session. You are totally protected by this aura of pure white light.

In a few moments I am going to count from 1 to 20. As I do so you will feel yourself rising up to the superconscious mind level where you will be able to receive information from your Masters and Guides. You will also be able to overview all of your past, present and future lives. Number 1 rising up. 2, 3, 4 rising higher. 5, 6, 7, letting information flow. 8, 9, 10, you are half way there. 11, 12, 13, feel yourself rising even higher. 14, 15, 16, almost there. 17,

18, 19 number 20 you are there. Take a moment and orient yourself to the superconscious mind level.

PLAY NEW AGE MUSIC FOR 1 MINUTE

Now slowly and carefully state your desire for information or an experience and let this superconscious mind level work for you.

Your Higher Self has all of the answers to the question what is my karmic purpose? Let your perfect component of your soul's energy assist you in learning why you chose this particular lifetime, and exactly what it is you are supposed to accomplish to complete this karmic subcycle. Ask your Higher Self to answer the question—"What is my karmic purpose?" Do this now.

PLAY NEW AGE MUSIC FOR 5 MINUTES

Let your superconscious mind now establish a complete and global communication and assessment of your karmic purpose. Begin with simple goals or purposes and move on to more advanced ones as you allow and encourage your Higher Self to let this information flow. You are raising your soul's frequency vibrational rate while this is occurring. Do this now.

PLAY NEW AGE MUSIC FOR 4 MINUTES

Alright now. Sleep now and rest. You did very very well. Listen very carefully. I'm going to count forwards now from 1-5. When I reach the count of 5 you will be back in the present, you will be able to remember everything you experienced and re-experienced you'll feel very relaxed refreshed, you'll be able to do whatever you have to planned for the rest of the day or evening. You'll feel very positive about what you've just experienced and very motivated about your confidence and ability to play this tape again to experience the superconscious mind level. Alright now. 1 very very deep, 2 you're getting a little bit lighter, 3 you're getting much much lighter, 4 very very light, 5 awaken. Wide awake and refreshed.

This next exercise incorporates the basic principles of affirmations, visual imagery and accessing the Higher Self to attain karmic capitalism:

Now listen very carefully. I want you to imagine a bright white light coming down from above and entering the top of your head. Filling your entire body. See it, feel it and it becomes reality. Now imagine an aura of pure white light emanating from your heart region. Again surrounding your entire body. Protecting you. See it, feel it and it becomes reality. Now only your masters and guides and highly evolved loving entities who mean you well will be able to influence you during this or any other hypnotic session. You are totally protected by this aura of pure white light.

In a few moments I am going to count from 1 to 20. As I do so you will feel yourself rising up to the superconscious mind level where you will be able to receive information from your Masters and Guides. You will also be able to overview all of your past, present and future lives. Number 1 rising up. 2, 3, 4 rising higher. 5, 6, 7, letting information flow. 8, 9, 10, you are half way there. 11, 12, 13, feel yourself rising even higher. 14, 15, 16, almost there. 17, 18, 19 number 20 you are there. Take a moment and orient yourself to the superconscious mind level.

PLAY NEW AGE MUSIC FOR 1 MINUTE

- I create my reality with complete positivity.
- I enjoy my life and create abundance daily.
- I succeed in all my endeavors.
- I love life and never compromise my ethics.
- Everyone I come into contact with teaches me something useful.
- I always expect the best from others and the universe.
- I love myself.
- I accept myself fully.
- I approve of myself fully.
- I'm capable of doing anything I want.
- I allow myself to experience the infinite intelligence of the universe through my Higher Self.
- I use the full capacity of my mind to manifest my life as I want it.
- I learn from every experience I have in my life.
- My past does not control my future, I do.
- I'm worthy of all the abundance the universe has to offer.
- I'm worthy of love.
- I trust the universe as a benevolent place that supports me in my abundance desires.
- I believe in people.
- I open myself to the universe.
- I take responsibility to create my life.
- I have the power to change my life.
- I make the choice to grow.
- I have created my past and I will create my future.
- I create my universe every day.
- I embrace changes as an essential ingredient in my growth process.
- There is nothing I cannot do, as the universe provides me with all of the raw materials for spiritual growth.
- My life is what I make it.
- My life is abundant with opportunities to contribute meaningfully to the world.

- I take responsibility to make the world a better place.
- I succeed in whatever I put my mind to.

Ask the following questions to your Higher Self regarding business issues:

1. What specific business problems are you dealing with that you would like resolved right now?

2. What outcome would you most like to achieve?

3. What karmic lesson is related to this situation?

4. What can you change about this situation with minimal effort? With a more significant commitment?

5. What one thing are you willing to change to obtain the resolution you would like?

6. How have you tried to resolve this situation so far?

7. What was it about this approach that did not work?

8. What is the ideal solution to this situation and focus in on how this could affect your professional life?

PLAY NEW AGE MUSIC FOR 3 MINUTES

Now state a specific business goal that represents what you truly want to achieve. This should be one that you deeply desire. Do not allow your current situation limit this goal. It should be positive, attainable, specific and relate to your training and experience.

You are creating a new belief, so it is important that this goal be somewhat beyond what you have accomplished so far in life, but not so distant that it would cause you to consider it unattainable.

Create a mental movie of yourself taking the appropriate steps to make this goal a reality. Incorporate emotions associated with the pride of attaining this goal, and anything else that represents positivity and spiritual growth. Focus on one dominating empowering image as you access your Higher Self with this mental movie. Perceive your own image receiving enjoyment and abundance from this visualization.

Always remember you are sending out your energy to accompany any idea that is created by your mind. The more positive your energy, the easier it will be to attain this abundance goal and the greater the chances of you accomplishing all that you set out to.

Finally, act as if this vision has already been accomplished following your daily self-hypnosis exercise. This is a form of giving credence and energy to your abundance desire. Speak to others, plan your actions and constantly think as if your vision is already a part of your new reality.

The forces of the universe manifested through your Higher Self will work with you in manifesting this visualization into an actual fact. You may observe this phenomena in the form of coincidences, which are actually synchronicities orchestrated by your Higher Self.

PLAY NEW AGE MUSIC FOR 5 MINUTES

You have done very well. Now I want you to further open up the channels of communication by removing any obstacles and allowing yourself to receive information and experiences that will directly apply to and help develop your ability to become a karmic capitalist. Allow yourself to receive more advanced and more specific information from your Higher Self and Masters and Guides to grow spiritually and improve your abundance. Do this now.

PLAY NEW AGE MUSIC FOR 4 MINUTES

Alright now. Sleep now and rest. You have done very well. Listen very carefully. I'm going to count forwards now from 1-5. When I reach the count of 5 you will return to your normal consciousness and be able to remember everything you experienced. You'll feel very relaxed refreshed, and you will be able to do whatever you have to planned for the rest of the day or evening. You'll feel very positive about what you've just experienced and very motivated about your confidence and ability to play this tape again to experience the superconscious mind level and to begin your life as a karmic capitalist. Number 1 very very deep, 2 you're getting a little bit lighter, 3 you're getting much much lighter, 4 very very light, 5 awaken. Wide awake and refreshed.

KARMIC CAPITALISM ON THE AIR

When I report examples of karmic capitalism from my own life, that of my patients or cases derived from outside sources, my intent is not just to illustrate abundance. Some form of spiritual growth or empowerment must accompany this material success for it to qualify as karmic capitalism.

Hypnosis is the modality I employ and teach all of my patients, simply because it works and is the most efficient method I have ever come across. In June 1997 I experienced what my colleagues and friends would call a whirlwind tour. The purpose of this three-and-a-half-day out-of-town trip was to conduct workshops in New York and attend the International New Age Trade Show (INATS) in Denver, representing my two Llewellyn books Soul Healing and The Search For Grace.

As is my pattern, I took a "redeye" flight from Los Angeles that left LAX at 10:00 P.M. on Thursday, June 27, and arrived at 6:10 A.M. at JFK in New York on June 28. During this flight I placed myself in a hypnotic trance and accessed my Higher Self for about one-and-a-half hours. This is not sleep per se, but provides my body with the equivalent of an eight hour rest.

With no sleep, I met with some media friends on Friday morning, conducted a 9:00 A.M. interview on a White Plains radio station on telephone and was interviewed on the Fox News channel at 11:40 A.M. (EST). My mind had to be alert, as this was a debate and my controversial position doesn't usually lend itself to warm fuzzies from news interviewers.

Following this interview I took a train to White Plains, New York to prepare for my workshop opening the Body, Mind and Soul Expo at the Westchester County Center. Just prior to my 7:00 P.M. workshop I saw a private patient, who experienced a major breakthrough with her spiritual blockages.

Immediately following my workshop and book signing, I again took a train to Grand Central Station, where I hailed a cab to take me to WOR Radio. Here I conducted an interview on the Joey Reynolds Show from 1:00 A.M. to 3:30 A.M. on network radio. This was my second consecutive night of no sleep! I did have an hour before the show to use my superconscious mind hypnotic nap.

Joey Reynolds is a great host. His New York persona, with his wit and charm, and his natural tendency to effectively promote the guest's book, was most appreciated.

During my superconscious mind tap just before Joey's show, my Higher Self suggested I guide the entire radio audience into their Higher Self and direct them to scan their past and future lives. Since I was promoting my books, Soul Healing and The Search For Grace, this technique was most appropriate.

In the past I have regressed and progressed hosts and producers live on the air, but not the entire audience. Joey was most receptive to the idea, and allowed me to conduct this group hypnotic experiment. During this exercise he went into trance himself. We received a call on the air from Frank from the Bronx who stated about his experience, "It was enlightening." Joey's comment at the end of another caller's question was, "Buy his book and then get back to me."

Greg from Houston reported, "I went through the experience with you and was able to visualize what you were speaking of. I'm going to buy your book." He was able to progress into the future of his current life.

Following this interview I went back to my hotel in White Plains for about two hours of a superconscious mind "nap" before my workshop and book signing. I left for the airport to fly to Denver at 2:30 P.M. for the INATS convention. It was 8:15 P.M. Denver time when I arrived at my hotel. The host of KTLK's 10:00 P.M. to midnight radio talk show, Elizabeth Ross, was kind enough to volunteer to drive me to her station for my interview with her.

On the air and near the end of the show a woman named Kate called in and described how she heard the Joey Reynold's Show earlier that day (KTLK is the Joey Reynold's Show affiliate in Denver) and was moved by my group hypnotic exercise, along with this synchronicity.

As I did this same exercise on KTLK, Kate had two exposures to her Higher Self in less than 24 hours, and was spiritually moved each time. My purpose in describing this trip is to illustrate that one can sell books and workshop tickets, yet at the same time assist others in their own spiritual growth. This is karmic capitalism.

Kate's synchronistic exposure to my work helped her. During the next few months I had the pleasure of working with several of Joey Reynold's listeners. One young man used my superconscious mind tape to assist him in an important business decision that was not only very lucrative, but it empowered him and helped his self-image so that he could switch to his entrepreneurial pursuit full time. That is what karmic capitalism is all about.

In practicing these self-hypnosis exercises, always bear in mind that you are cooperating with the way the universe functions. By creating a goal in your mind, focusing your soul's energy on its realization and acting as if it has been attained you are assisting the process of the unfoldment of your dream.

CHAPTER 6

REPOWERMENT VS EMPOWERMENT

Empowerment is defined as taking charge of your life. By eliminating the neediness, shoulds and codependencies, an empowered soul becomes an optimistic, confident leader directing their own life and functioning as an effective role model for others.

The corporate world has been using this term quite a bit to train executives and entrepreneurs in attaining abundance. I would like to introduce the concept of repowerment. By repowerment I am implying all of the precepts established by empowerment, with one exception. The difference between repowerment and empowerment is that in the former we are regaining talents and abilities we once had, but either repressed or discarded.

I honestly feel that our very soul is naturally empowered. We wouldn't have survived as a species during the past 100,000 years if we weren't. Society has conditioned, if not brainwashed, us to scale down this innate instinct. The very existence of civilization, with all of its bureaucracies would be threatened it the people who are controlled by it were too independent and empowered.

It is our right and responsibility as a soul to take back this natural component of karmic capitalism. Never lose track of the principle that all "problems" are merely disguised opportunities. The universe is actually completely supportive of your quest to become repowered.

For those of you who do not share the concept that the universe is on your side, you either are allowing your past frustrations to unduly scar you, or have not learned the lessons that your soul selected for you in this lifetime.

A certain amount of trust and faith in this perfect system must be exhibited by you in order to allow this spiritual unfoldment to occur. We are all presented with circumstances and the raw materials necessary to achieve our objectives. With karmic capitalism these goals are easier to attain, since a spiritual growth path is one of its main components.

You may choose an approach that does not reflect karmic capitalism to attain abundance. However, if you seek material goals through selfish manipulation of others, your spiritual unfoldment will be blocked. The very goals you desire will be elusive. Even if you do become wealthy, your personal life will be miserable. My Los Angeles office is filled with patients who represent the rich, powerful but miserable.

THE EMPOWERMENT CYCLE

When you exhibit the discipline to practice accessing your Higher Self daily, an unlocking of an energy flow will be felt by you. This channeling of the perfect energy from your Higher Self results in a greater feeling of self-confidence and higher levels of creativity. These, in turn, opens up your intuitive powers and functions to resist the defense mechanism's natural tendency to detour you from attaining spiritual growth.

A positive upward spiral of empowerment now becomes incorporated into your daily subconscious programming. Each day it will become easier and easier to accept this new you. Abundance now manifests in your reality as the new you replaces the former you. Fear is overcome, and you have now established the basis of transforming yourself into a karmic capitalist.

FEAR IS FINALLY CONQUERED

The karmic capitalist knows no fear or insecurity. Since fear is a destructive and limiting state of mind, it is the result of poor programming. The emotion we label as fear is eliminated once the subconscious is properly reprogrammed. It is our interpretation of the world around us that results in fear being generated. Fear is an uneasiness of the mind composed of thoughts and usually an exaggeration of reality.

We acquire fear through our use of imagination in transforming neutral factors in our environment to an anxiety provoking stimulus. Fear now becomes a force that brings on self-defeating sequences as a dysfunctional response to this situation. Since whatever the mind can conceive, it can achieve, we can use hypnosis to remove fears. This is part of our psychic empowerment.

Even when circumstances become such that a certain setback is inevitable in our business life, the empowered karmic capitalist taps into his or her reserves of inner strength (Higher Self) and devices a way to both learn from this bit of misfortune and rise above any potential negative effects.

Becoming a karmic capitalist entails repowering your soul to encourage the world to move to a higher level of growth – an enlightenment. You now join other spiritually evolved souls as part of a global network assisting with this paradigm. While this is happening, you also become wealthy. That is karmic capitalism at its best.

The challenges you face and the goals your soul envisions will be within your range of attainment. Through the use of synchronicities and the assistance of other spiritually evolved souls, these visions will become your new reality. This system is reflective of your self-worth.

The value you place upon yourself will always reflect your soul's growth and inner consciousness. A poverty mentality will severely limit your ability to attract success and keep it. By recognizing the importance your own spiritual unfoldment has to the universe as a whole, any fears will be removed and your path to abundance cleared of unnecessary obstacles.

All of these principles require faith in yourself and your Higher Self. When you love yourself and unconditionally have faith in the universe, you take the single most important step in the direction of becoming a karmic capitalist.

These leaps of faith are critical if we are to transform the corporate world into one of ubiquitous karmic capitalism. A spiritual awakening is on the horizon as we enter a new millennium. We are about to witness a new era of the business age, a repowerment of entire industries!

To engage in this paradigm on a massive scale entails calling upon inner resources as never before utilized. This may appear to be in opposition to all our culturally derived notions of what is required to be successful. MBA programs may not be training graduate students in business to access their Higher Self, but a competitive edge does exist in spiritual approaches to business. The market will then decide who survives, who fails and which individuals and companies thrive.

We see phases in the business cycle, such as recession and expansion and bull and bear markets. Eventually there is a balance because the universe functions by way of opposing forces. A repowerment results from the dynamic tension between these opposing forces.

In the West action-oriented behaviors, such as drive, achievement and goal setting dominate, and results in an imbalance that eventually leads to a down phase in the business cycle. The ancients have always taught balance, a receiving and releasing opposing force to the Western traits previously mentioned.

Repowerment results when the forces of action and receptivity are properly balanced within each of us, as within a company or other system. The I Ching teaches us that everything is in constant movement, strengthening or weakening on a continual basis. When any particular quality gets strong enough, it eventually peaks–turning into its opposite (as the Ying/Yang symbol depicts). Each quality, according to ancient Chinese philosophy, contains its opposite.

From the depths of recession in the business cycle growth and expansion originate. Instead of practicing a useless form of resistance, if we work within the system and learn when to retreat early in a down phase, our business losses will be cut.

Exceptional modesty and conscientiousness are rewarded with success by the universe. Compare this to the chest-beating arrogance exhibited by many Western businesspeople. Always view your strengths and weaknesses objectively. Use your Higher Self to perform what I term a global assessment. This objective overview also includes directing yourself to fulfill your karmic purpose, while perceiving yourself or a business proposal without emotion. When humility is seen as part of the natural cycle of life, you begin to understand how, why, and when your own shortcomings can turn into your great virtue.

As a dental student I had to work my way through school the only job I cold find that allowed me to study, paid reasonably well and was logistically convenient was that of a security guard. Upon applying for this position I honestly informed the personnel director that I had absolutely no experience. The other four candidates were all seasoned veterans and were interviewed prior to me.

When I entered the personnel director's office and completed my interview, I was hired right on the spot. This was great news, but my curiosity peaked as to why I was chosen over the more qualified candidates. The director informed me that anyone can learn the specifics of functioning as a security guard. What was more desirable was my honesty, humility and obvious willingness to learn.

In applying repowerment principles and global assessment techniques it is important to recognize when you are in over your head. Sometimes your skills and experience fall short of that required for a particular position or project. When you perceive this, simply ally yourself with someone who can make this goal happen. Your growth is facilitated by the fact that you learned how to accomplish this task, and are seen as a humble team player.

Leadership likes humble team players, and are more likely to view your attitude and work favorably because of this trait of karmic capitalism.

Accessing your Higher Self on a regular basis initiates an intuitive process that directs you toward the right and best way to handle business decisions and actions. Always look for the good in others and, more often than not, you will attract them into your sphere of influence.

It is only by cultivating an appreciation for the full cycle of positive and negative forces that you will be led to opportunities resulting in fulfillment and abundance. For example, if you desire a certain position in your company that there are currently no openings for, train yourself to do this job and act as if you attained this higher level title. Become the person who represents that particular job, and use your Higher Self to effect this change in your belief system. This places you more directly on the path to making this goal your reality more so than any conventional paradigm you can apply.

Always place your major emphasis in your business goals in the dictates of your own heart. Following your inner convictions after you have mastered the superconscious mind tap will repower both you and your associates, and more efficiently result in the attainment of the abundance you so desire.

Each and every day you should be developing your character. Perseverance, honesty, strength and faith are among those traits that need to be cultivated the most. The universe will then bring into your realm those individuals who represent these same characteristics. Never run away from your limitations. Recognize them, work on them and encourage others to do likewise.

Reclaim your power. That is what repowerment is all about. The mirror of karma principle has many applications. Emulate an example of a person doing what you wish to do, until you develop your own style. However, observing someone in your life doing something that you abhor should immediately orient you to search within your own soul for this very fault or tendency.

Always be forthright and conscientious about doing what your heart tells you is the correct thing. Look for opportunities to be of service to others. Be open and accessible to the feedback and opinion of others. Make a total commitment to speaking the truth at all times and doing what is right. When the universe is prepared for you to move forward, an opportunity for abundance will present itself.

HOW A KARMIC CAPITALIST APPLIES FOR A JOB

Before I detail a simple method of obtaining a position you desire, consider how effective you are at communicating with others. Listen to yourself by holding your left hand over your left ear to hear the way others receive your voice. Try recording a conversation with your family, friends or business associate.

Next, play back this tape to objectively evaluate your speech patterns and style of communication. If you repeatedly say "you know or "uh-huh," these need to be worked on. Listen to the rate at which you speak. Many people talk too quickly and would get points across more effectively by slowing down. Use inflection—practice raising or lowering your pitch for emphasis.

After you have corrected problems with communication skills, it is time to prepare for that job interview. When seeking a new job, you have only about one minute to make a good first impression. Begin this process by discussing what you do best. Present an example of a time when you excelled at your job skills. Practice this speech with friends or family for feedback. The length of this presentation will vary depending on various factors. Use your Higher Self's judgment for this and other critical issues.

If you telephone a prospective employer allow them to do most of the talking. This is a test of your ability to be an effective listener, as well as communicator. Only make or receive this call when you are emotionally ready and have properly prepared for this screening.

Here are some additional traits you need to possess in order to be successful in pursuits leading to a job that will allow you to become a karmic capitalist:

1. You must have a clear purpose, such as personal growth, making a contribution to society, learning or some other goal in order to locate a high-paying, high-integrity job.

2. A willingness to work hard for what you want is also required. I refer to this as internal motivation. This entails a high level of assertiveness, persistence and creativity. You will need to learn all about job interviews, job-search and apply these principles conscientiously.

3. The will to meet your goal also needs to be exhibited by you on a daily basis. Weak intention leads to procrastination and lack of focus. These promote limiting beliefs about yourself and your ability to attain this goal.

4. A high level of conscious awareness must be exercised during this search. All robotic-like behaviors must be extinguished, and your

subconscious needs to be easily accessible to assure your success. Whenever possible, always deal directly with the person who has the authority to hire you. Be prepared for the unexpected.

5.   A recognition as to when you have found your ideal position must be acknowledged. You are the only person capable of judging whether your goals have been met. With the help of your Higher Self, you can finally achieve inner fulfillment to accompany the outer rewards offered by abundance.

HOW A KARMIC CAPITALIST DEALS WITH DIFFICULT BUSINESSPEOPLE

The natural tendency is to escalate a conflict with an individual who is either argumentative, or just downright annoying. This response is a defense mechanism reflex and only achieves alienation and dysfunctional responses.

You will never change another person or prove them wrong by attacking them. The karmic capitalist acts from both a spiritual and rational perspective. Always place yourself in this individual's shoes and try to discern their needs. This technique places you in a problem-solving mode and allows a healthy distance between you and them.

Do not take this person's psychological problems personally. They act this way with everyone. I do not advocate you pity them either. They karmically chose this pattern in their life. Work with them and demonstrate compassion. You would be surprised how fast they can respond positively to your caring attitude. Use the superconscious mind tape to assist you in preventing your emotions from taking over your responses.

There are six main categories of difficult people in business. Here is a breakdown of these types and how to effectively deal with them:

1.   The Procrastinator. These types are obsessed by perfectionism, or by the belief that they are not in a position to ask for help. The best way to deal with them is to brainstorm different methods of resolving the problem.

2.   The Weasel. This individual uses humor to disguise their criticism of you. They will also take credit for your work behind your back, or simply gossip about you. It is critical to expose these tactics in front of your co-workers. Saying things such as, "Was that negative remark directed at me?" or "I hate to break the news to you, but I proposed that very idea last week." Always present hard evidence (memos, taped conversations, etc.) to support your contentions.

3. The Bully. A bully tries to bulldoze his or her way upon others or by venting their arsenal of neuroses. When this person has completed their outburst, calmly state your point of view and act as if the outburst never occurred. You will most likely have to concede on some minor points to allow them to save face and defuse their aggressiveness.

4. The Negativist. He or she constantly finds flaws in every idea you propose. The best way to handle this cynic is to confront them on their being against any alternatives. This should be done in the company of decision makers on the team. A negativist fears failure above all. Follow up your assertive response with a compassionate reassurance that you are competent to deal with any problems that may arise from your suggestions.

5. The Depressed Type. A depressed businessperson acts distant and lethargic without revealing why they feel this way. The karmic capitalist asks open-ended questions, such as "How do you feel about this proposal?" Patience is required here, as there will be periods of silence. Refrain from filling up this silence. It will most likely require several efforts to ascertain the cause of their mood.

6. The Whiner. A whiner constantly complains. They feel powerless and assume nobody listens to them, or cares about their views. A karmic capitalist uses reflective listening methods. This consists of repeating back to this individual what you heard them say in your own words. An effective technique is to validate their complaint and shift your focus on problem solving efforts.

The universe is not created for yours or my pleasure. It only shows concern for your development and growth as a soul. Such qualities as compassion, faith, forgiveness and patience are character traits that allow for the highest expression of yourself.

Any obstacle you face in life is presented by the universe to strengthen your character, not to punish you. Never whine and complain about your lot in life. Look within your own mirror of karma and globally assess the situation with the aid of your Higher Self. Then do what is necessary to move forward. If you are bored in life, set a higher goal.

A karmic capitalist uses their ability to demonstrate repowerment in dealing with stress. Pressure is what we put on ourselves when we set high standards for excellence and we struggle to meet or exceed those standards. This is actually quite healthy and is an important component of karmic capitalism. Stress, on the other hand, is negative energy that is caused by external forces when we're not focused or prepared for challenges. Burnout can result from too much stress.

We want to have a certain amount of pressure in life to stimulate our best efforts. Even if the outcome is less than your expectations, you will feel better about yourself, because you gave 120 percent. Although you can't control the world, you can control your frame of mind. Focus on the upside of any difficult task or job assignment.

Completing half of this goal should now generate a more positive attitude towards the remainder of this assignment. The pessimist's cup is half empty. The optimist's cup is half full. Overflowing is how I describe the cup of the karmic capitalist.

Repowerment has many specific applications to karmic capitalism. Here are some new ways of functioning in the business world that indicate you have undergone repowerment.

• All feedback given and received is from a constructive versus defensive perspective.

• You show your true feelings when dealing with your staff. You always say what you mean and mean what you say.

• Each matter is decided upon with complete objectivity and fairness, as if your judgment could save someone's life.

• Even though an individual doesn't trust you, you exhibit patience, humility, understanding and compassion toward them.

Your business life will improve by way of attractive opportunities the moment you cease demanding peaks from your career. The more you give to others and the universe, the more you receive in return. "What goes around comes around."

There are times when you need to quit your "straight job" and devote full time to your entrepreneurial pursuits. Many people exhibit guilt when this day arrives. This negative feeling is sometimes projected by your employer, who wants you to stay for more selfish reasons. Here are some principles that will assist you in breaking away from these corporate apron strings and still grow spiritually:

• Leave your company if you honestly feel that you have built up rather than diminished the legacy of those who preceded you.

• Feel confident to start your own business if your Higher Self informs you that this choice is better for the universe.

• Do not leave the company if your "grub stake" is based on resources, contacts and so on that belong to the company. If these are your own resources, welcome to entrepreneurial karmic capitalism.

• Feel confident about your decision to leave the corporate structure if the standard you created in the company is one that you would want your son or daughter to emulate.

Build your new company on a principle that reflects your spiritual side. Companies built on adversarial and ruthless paradigms are continually at war with someone, or themselves. Vital, win-in-win, compassionate corporations have low turnover, high morale, more profits and add to the quality of the universe.

Never feel insecure about placing trust in the universe. We all must take a leap of faith at times in our professional lives. I most certainly did that when I gave up a lucrative dental practice to devote full time attention to my hypnotherapy career.

Always live a highly ethical life in all aspects. Be proud of everything you do and who you are. Never allow fear into your life. Be human, but spiritual. Stay on the road to self-improvement with an equally open mind and heart. Be a repowered karmic capitalist.

CHAPTER 7

WHAT DOES KARMIC CAPITALISM MEAN TO ME?

THE VICIOUS CYCLE OF WORKING

The main reason I decided to write this book was to show how we can all attain abundance and grow spiritually at the same time. One of the biggest problems in Western society today is that our relationship with money has taken over the major part of our lives.

We spend well over 40 hours out of each 168 hours that comprises a week earning a living. When we are not actually working, we think about our jobs at home. Often mindless forms of entertainment designed to assist us in escapism is sought to "recreate" from these vocations.

Once or twice a year we "vacate" our positions and occasionally require attention from health professionals to deal with the stress from these professional encounters. Some of our spare time is occupied by job seminars or company social events which furthers this work obsession.

In order to keep up with the Joneses, we spend money on our home, car, clothes and other luxuries to reflect our status in the work world.

Another problem we face in the business world is identifying too much with our jobs. A worker who takes care of your lawn doesn't say "I do gardening." He or she states, "I am a gardener." If we are not overly identifying with our jobs, we are functioning as consumers. The dictionary definition of consume is to destroy or use up. Is it no wonder that consumption based businesses and economies have absolutely nothing to do with karmic capitalism?

Too much of our time is devoted to earning a living in order to buy more luxuries. We simply don't take the necessary time to properly examine our priorities. Spiritual growth should be at the very top of that priority list.

The old thought in business and our attitude toward money has led us into a web of financial dependencies. From birth to death we have become financially dependent—on our parents for our first financial sustenance, on "the economy" in order to get a good job after graduation, on "the job" for our survival, on "unemployment" hand outs to tide us over between jobs, on our corporate pension to pay our way in old age, on Social Security to supplement our corporate pension and on Medicare or Medicaid if we get stick before we die. Even with all of this obsession with money, 95 percent of Americans who reach the age of 65 are living at poverty levels of income, being almost totally dependent on Social Security or relatives to survive.

This old thought system simply does not work. It entails absolutely no spiritual growth, and results in poverty lifestyles upon retirement. Karmic capitalism allows you to choose and design your own path, and to integrate abundance with the rest of your life on the road to spiritual growth.

The classic paradigms concerning money have resulted in the following circumstances for most Americans:

- Requiring two paychecks to make ends meet.
- Not liking your job, but not having a viable alternative.
- Spending more than you earn.
- Being so confused by money that you leave it to the experts, who in turn take advantage of your ignorance.
- Taking no time for spirituality, so life has no real meaning or purpose beyond paying bills.

Merely reading this book will do little to change your consciousness and beliefs about money and personal growth. You must practice the simple exercises I present to get in touch with your Higher Self and reprogram your subconscious. This will lead to a transformation in regards to your relationship with money, which in turn will generate abundance accompanied by spirituality.

Some examples of benefits my patients report following the application of the principles and exercises presented in this book are:

- An integration between money and the rest of their life.
- Improved relationships with their mates and children.
- More free time to pursue interests that lead to a better overall balance in their life.
- An elimination of obsession with money.
- The development of a higher level of integrity in all aspects of their life.
- Better communication skills in general.
- A more fulfilling and less stressful life.

•   New and innovative solutions are discovered for life's challenges. In the past they would simply buy their way out of "problems."

MONETARY PARADIGMS

There are several ways of looking at money and abundance. As we grow spiritually, there is a natural tendency to focus less on the insecurity of not having enough money to a form of psychic empowerment that allows us to enjoy life and comprehend our karmic purpose and our place in the universe.

Here are some examples of monetary views:

1.   The practical view of money. An everyday concept of money deals with the various financial transactions that characterize our lives. This includes our developmental belief system from the first allowance we may have received as a child to our first paying job.

Included in this paradigm are the principles of money management. We are educated as to the different types of bank accounts, how to apply for a mortgage, car loan, etc. Balancing our checking account, the different forms of investment vehicles (stocks, municipal bonds, Fannie Maes, Sallie Maes and Freddie Macs futures, options, junk bonds, real estate and so on) retirement plans, insurance credit cards and trust funds.

This view quite simply represents the entire range of dealings and concerns with money from the simplest information to the most sophisticated formulas that we encounter during our lives. The problem that begins to surface at this juncture is a growing "more is better" mentality encouraged by consumer-driven non-karmic capitalistically run corporations. We tend to shop for new goods if we are dissatisfied with our car, home, clothes, electronic gadgets or other items. Much of this compulsive spending is related to our insecurities of keeping up with the Joneses.

The real danger that occurs at this time is buying on credit and overextending ourselves financially. When those monthly credit card bills arrive, many Americans only pay the interest. The principal keeps accumulating, and this leads to a vicious cycle of financial panic versus compulsive spending.

People caught in the financial web now limit their options and never seem to question whether or not the game is worth playing at all or whether there might be a better game to play. They say things to me such as, "Whenever I make ends meet someone moves the other end." These individuals have no concept of finding healthy solutions for their financial woes. Every time they devise a way out of their dilemma, another problem appears.

Examples of this non-spiritual, immature and responsible approach to abundance is represented by the typical American stock market investor. These non-karmic capitalists base their decisions on hunches, whims, what they should have done last week, what their broker tells them and their own uneducated assessment of the future.

Inevitably, they lose money with this behavior, but refuse to take a step back and globally assess their situation. Instead, they decide they should buy more stock, a better stock or a different stock so that they can recoup their losses. This same useless approach is applied at casinos during vacations when these individuals dogmatically assume that if they just keep gambling, all of the money they lost will be regained.

2.   The psychological view of money. This view concerning abundance represents the first "nonmaterial" level of money, the emotional interactions with money. This is the level of our personal thoughts and feelings about money—our money style or personality. Your tendency to be competitive, generous, miserly, cautious, impulsive, snobbish, a worrier and so on illustrate this monetary psychological profile. At this point in our lives we come to see how our own attitudes about money were shaped by the psychological environment we grew up in.

The person in charge of financial affairs in your family, their feelings toward abundance, the belief that your family had enough money to buy you anything you desired, associating money with rewards or control ("purse-string" approaches) and never seeing your father or mother because of their work schedule are some of the factors that may have contributed to your monetary psychological profile.

An awareness of your psychological orientation toward money can assist you in making better choices in the practical aspects of daily abundance issues. Monetary issues account for the vast majority of divorces, so your relationships can be markedly improved by adopting karmic capitalistic paradigms.

Included in this psychological view of money are what money specifically means to us. This is what I refer to as the monetary myths. Here are some examples of monetary myths:

A.   Money buys social standing. The desire to keep up with the Joneses is an insecurity characterized by a profound desire to be accepted socially. From spending money to entertaining friends, family members, business associates and clients, society perpetrates the concept that this superficial expression of our low self-image is actually going to truly impress others.

I do not doubt that equally insecure and superficial people may be at least temporarily impressed by your monetary expenditure, but in the long run there is no spiritual growth, and therefore no karmic capitalism.

Another form of social acceptance offered us by money is our own personal appearance and hygiene. Madison Avenue's very successful brainwashing of the American public is represented by products that make us look thinner (diets), look sexier (clothes, cars, alcohol), smell better from head (shampoos) to toe (foot powder) and stay in step with the "in crowd" by purchasing the latest gadgets on the market.

We even fall prey to the old medieval concept of money as the basis of marriage contracts. Do we not apply the principle that money will attract the opposite sex? This myth fosters the view that money equals acceptance.

Companionship, friendship and intimacy are all available free of charge to people who sincerely extend their love to others. It's when we equate money with social acceptance that the distortions begin. There is no joy in spending money to gain acceptance but never experiencing true intimacy. The karmic capitalist always encounters true bliss in their lives, since their spirituality obviates the insecurities implied by a codependence on money to establish status.

B.   Money is a source of power. You can attain and exercise a form of power with money, such as "purse-string" manipulation of others, but those on the receiving end will most likely despise you and rebel at any available moment. Purse string mentality refers to the giving or withholding of money to command compliance and loyalty from those dependent on him or her— family, employees, favorite charities and so on.

You may wholeheartedly disagree with my denying that money represents true power. Can you not go where you want to, do something you desire or pay someone else to perform a chore you didn't care to do yourself? These are true statements, but did not the Roman Empire collapse because of the practice of its citizens hiring mercenaries to fulfill their military obligations?

Another example of how true power has nothing to do with money is represented by the liberation of India from British rule by Gandhi. Gandhi called his power satyagraha, or "soul force." When faced with the indomitable determination of Gandhi and his followers, the British government finally gave up its colonial rule of this vast nation of India and granted it independence.

Gandhi's soul power was a form of spirituality expressed by extremely poor people, whose lives were characterized by irrepressible job. They may not have been karmic capitalists, but they illustrated the spiritual components of this paradigm and obtained their freedom from a far more powerful and influential nation.

C.   Money as security. For many people security is having money in the bank and a stable earning position so that they can always get more. This spectrum includes penny-pinching (denying themselves not only luxuries but the necessities of life) to compulsive spending (buy now, buy ore, buy two) to compulsive saving. Some of these souls mistakenly equate financial security with emotional security. Money is used to deal with unpleasant emotional states like fear, worry, anxiety and loneliness through buying companions, bodyguards, accountants, friends, memberships in country clubs, therapists and worst of all drugs, and other escapist solutions to these woes. The belief that money represents security is one of the most common myths in society.

D.   Money as the root of all evil. The biblical admonition that "the love of money is the root of all evil" has been one of the most dominant factors in creating this myth. It is quite simply our attachment to things over people that pushes us into wrong action. Money doesn't perpetuate evil to others—we commit evil acts. Money isn't evil, dirty or any other trait. It is morally neutral. The only way money can harm others results from our addiction to it and our insecurities as reflected by possessiveness, jealousy and control issues.

3.   The karmic capitalist view of money. When you adopt the principles of karmic capitalism, your attitude toward abundance will be transformed into a spiritually-based paradigm characterized by psychic empowerment, feelings of bliss, unlimited creativity and self-confidence and levels of fulfillment you could only dream about now.

To reevaluate your current attitude and beliefs toward money today, consider these three questions, and answer them honestly.

A.   Is what I do for a living meaningful to me and my karmic purpose?

B.   Do I obtain joy, satisfaction and fulfillment from my work that is in proportion to the time, energy and emotions I expend?

C.   If I didn't have to work to support myself and my family, what would be the best use of my time that would add to the quality of the universe?

The spectrum of negative emotions, such as fear, guilt, frustration, boredom and other examples of emotional imbalance occur when your actions are out of alignment with your values. These unwanted feelings may be eliminated by doing one of two things. You can alter your actions to align with your values, and function like a true karmic capitalist, or you can change your values to align with your actions. This second approach is what I term the "down-a-later" paradigm. By following this philosophy you enter a bottomless fjord of compromises and "soul selling" to rationalize your behavior.

The true karmic capitalist awakens within themselves (by accessing their Higher Self) a natural and spiritual sense of knowing when enough is enough. Refer back to the top of the consumption curve labeled as enough to visualize this concept.

Karmic capitalists easily differentiate between a passing fancy and real fulfillment, that point of perfect balance where desires disappear because they have been completely met. Any less would be not enough. Any more would be too much. An internal sense of awareness now rejects any superficial desires to impress others. There now is practiced a principle that if a purchase or experience is truly fulfilling, the desire disappears for a long time. You are satisfied and free of the humiliation of being manipulated into spending your life energy on things that don't bring you fulfillment.

FINDING OUR KARMIC PURPOSE

Daily practice with the superconscious mind tape will place you in touch with your Higher Self and open your mind to receive your true mission in this life that I refer to as your karmic purpose. It is only given to you when you are spiritually ready to receive it. You must raise the quality of your soul's energy (cleansing) to attain this vital data.

Our karmic purpose represents even more than a passionate commitment to abundance. It relates to our relationships with others and a desire to make the world a better place to live –perhaps helping solve problems of hunger, homelessness, abusive family relationships or global warming. Sometimes a person's mission is to embody certain qualities, such as love, peace or nonviolence. You do not have to be a Gandhi or Mother Teresa to exhibit these qualities.

There are some simple practices you can incorporate in your daily life to speed up your spiritual growth and align your soul with its karmic purpose. Here are some examples:

1.   Engage in occupations that allow you to work form your heart. This form of healing can range from offering others your wisdom and compassion to charity work. You may achieve this by contributing large sums of money

to quality organizations, assisting others (such as Project Hope, the Red Cross), UNICEF and others.

2.   Work with what enters your universe. There are many opportunities that present themselves by responding to the needs of others. This principle illustrates the interconnectedness of the world. There is no single act of greatness, just a series of small acts done with great passion or great love.

3.   Involve yourself with what your soul directs you to. This means focusing your attention on projects that you care deeply about. When you look for something you love more than your own comfort and convenience, you are well on your way to finding your karmic purpose. Think about what you would like to do if you weren't paid for it and you were financially independent. Meditating on this while playing your superconscious mind tape will orient you in this direction.

An accurate measure of whether you are living your karmic purpose—one that goes beyond material success and beyond rewards and recognition, is your answer to the question "Is this expenditure of life energy in alignment with my values?" Living in alignment with your stated karmic purpose is your true purpose.

CONSPICUOUS CONSUMPTION

When you spend money for the purpose of impressing others, you are functioning from a perspective of ego and insecurity. Your efforts are most likely not even going to be noticed by others, since they are probably too busy trying to impress you or other individuals.

This is what is Thorstein Veblen termed "conspicuous consumption," and is both a historical and cross-cultural phenomenon. Just think of all of the time, energy and money you will save by following the principles of karmic capitalism, rather than conspicuous consumption. Again, refer back to the two consumption curves I presented earlier.

Conspicuous consumption represents one of the favorite capitalistic highs of Americans. It is an unhealthy addiction that is sanctioned by non-karmic corporate capitalists who feed into the consumption-driven paradigm that is the opposite of what corporate karmic capitalism represents, as we shall see in the next chapter.

THE PURPOSES OF WORK

Work has two different functions: the material, financial function (i.e., getting paid) and the personal function (emotional, intellectual, psychological and spiritual). Here is a more comprehensive list of what working provides us with:

- New skills.
- Recognition of our value to society.
- An opportunity to socialize with others in a hopefully meaningful way.
- An opportunity to receive respect, admiration and praise for others and society in general.
- An environment to be challenged and express our creativity and expertise.
- A sense of empowerment and influence over the course of events, products or services resulting from commerce.
- Structuring our time to provide discipline and a rhythm to our lives.
- Continuing a tradition established either with a family business or with a certain name brand product or discipline.
- Providing a service to others, society and the world.
- An opportunity to strive for success.
- A source of income to take care of the necessities of life, comforts, luxuries, philanthropic goals and to provide for our heirs.
- Establishing a foundation for spiritual growth.

If we think that what we do to make money is who we are, we will end up adopting whatever pattern will allows us to survive best at our job. By keeping separate who you are as a unique soul and what your professional responsibilities are, you can reclaim your lost identity and psychically empower yourself.

This allows us to work at our jobs without losing ourselves in the process. By following the ancient's advice of "know thyself," you come to know yourself, your values, your beliefs, your real talents and what you care about, you will be able to work from the perspective of your Higher Self, rather than your ego. If any job you engage in does not allow for this, leave it as soon as possible.

There is growing evidence that upwardly mobile professionals are voluntarily taking cuts in pay in order to live a more balanced life in alignment with their karmic purpose. Amy Saltzman, author of

Downshifting: Reinventing Success on a Slower Track, directs attention to those people who altered their professional lives in order to find their life purpose and obtain greater meaning for their being.

The ancient Greeks viewed their leisure time as an opportunity for self-development and exploration of their highest purpose. It is time we approach our leisure time with the same reverence.

Michael Phillips discusses the concept of "right livelihood," which he defines as an occupation that represents your true work purpose and financially supports you at the same time. To engage in this right livelihood, we must follow our
heart and soul.

He presents his thesis in his book, The Seven Laws of Money, and proposes that by changing our behavior system to eliminate the expectation that we will be remunerated for work that represents our true passion, we can then earn a living without compromise, develop more integrity and attract such a vocation into our life.

He points out traps people fall into when they attempt to accomplish this dual objective. He states:

"Unfortunately, many people can't separate the two, and the net result is that their belief that the project they are working on is the most important thing they can do gets coupled with their conviction that they have to survive. The combination of these two ideas leads them to believe that the world owes them a living."

You need to evaluate carefully all potential career choices in your quest for right livelihood. Bear in mind that any activity that is either publicly or privately funded is subject
to someone else's whims and priorities. Any product or service that depends on a fickle consuming public might not survive in a competitive marketplace. This is where accessing your Higher Self prior to making your choice will protect you from any potential Trojan horses in the universe.

Removing the expectation that the world owes you a living opens your mind up to receiving opportunities that will lead you to discover your true work and karmic purpose. This break in the link between work and money actually functions to give you back your life.

Let me describe what karmic capitalism is not. It is not merely "catching the wave" of fame and fortune. Too often we read about an actor who finally lands a hit television series or feature film, and then spends more time in a drug rehabilitation unit or jail than they do on the set.

The professional athlete or corporate executive who also cannot handle their material success with some extreme form of dysfunctional behavior is another sad example of catching the wave without accompanying this phenomenon with spiritual growth.

By practicing karmic capitalism principles, you will quickly learn to tap into your own inner resources (Higher Self) to free up the limitations that in the past may have prevented you from attaining abundance. You will learn the art and power of creating your reality, the life you now only dream about, by boldly and courageously reaching for your highest visions and attaining them.

Learning how to harness the passion of your heart and the power of your mind, while creating your fullest expression of being human is my definition of psychic empowerment, and a component of karmic capitalism.

You will discover what it is you really want for and in your life and avoid years spent pursuing other people's dreams. You will learn how to see and create a compelling vision of the life you truly desire. You will learn how to overcome those parts of yourself that can sabotage your intentions (self-defeating sequences). You will learn techniques to remove disabling attitudes and bring your life vision into full manifestation.

Never look to society as a model of functional behavior and paradigms. Our culture focuses on what is wrong with a person. Many therapies consider success to be helping people get "better," with "better" being defined as the absence of neurosis. Rarely is there a direct focus on full potential or optimum well-being, least of all spiritual growth as a foundation for attaining abundance. Following society's brainwashing results in each of learning merely how to cope and fit in rather than to excel and reach our spiritual heights.

To create a vision for your professional and personal life you must develop an acute awareness of the possibilities that lie within your true inner self (your Higher Self). This requires you to overcome all previous obstacles represented by limitations and false beliefs, and to be open to discover and manifest your fullest possibility as a human being (a child of the universe).

Learning how to transform limiting beliefs and behavior patterns, how to overcome difficult life situations and problems, not as ends in themselves but as part of the process of self-creation requires shifting our basic attitude toward life from problem-solving to vision-creating. Now you can release your creative energies and direct them toward achieving what you really want—from a healthier body to material success to greater connection with your Higher Self.

MOTIVATIONS FOR KARMIC CAPITALISM

We all need reasons to make major changes in our lives. Consider the following list of motivations for developing yourself as a karmic capitalist, a starting point in moving in this direction:

- The desire to learn about my true purpose.
- An interest in applying my personal and spiritual growth to the workplace.
- The desire to eliminate self-defeating sequences from my life once and for all.
- The desire to become balanced in body, mind and spirit.
- A true yearning for spirituality.
- The desire to eliminate obsessive worrying and to learn how to focus and attain my goals.
- The desire to acquire and hold onto money.
- The desire for psychic empowerment.

One of the most common characteristics of Westerners today is their devotion to a tremendous amount of energy (body and soul) to providing for their external needs (home, family, etc.) that they ignore their inner life of connection to the true spiritual part of their being (Higher Self). This obsession with actively "doing" things, rather than "being" (a receptive state), is one of the main obstacles to spiritual growth.

We need to learn the art of being to both access and nourish our inner awareness. This establishes a balance between our outer and inner life. It is not uncommon to experience feelings and sensations of wonder, reverence and bliss during these altered states of consciousness (ASCs).

This voyage of self-discovery is a most exciting and challenging experience. Most of us have not entered this path with proficiency because of a lack of a clear goal and no understanding of the simple methods for creating this journey. You must always know what it is you desire and how to realize it to attain any abundance and spiritual goal.

The techniques presented in chapter 5 instruct you in how to use your mind to create what you want for your life and developing the personal power to sustain your growth over time. We discussed in chapter 4 the limiting beliefs that prevent spiritual growth and abundance. Unhealthy beliefs sabotage your natural ability to grow spiritually. Healthy core beliefs provide an ideal environment for this growth.

The following chart describes a healthy core belief system that promotes karmic capitalism:

ASPECT OF LIFE
CORE BELIEF

Focused concentration
Emotions
Relationships
Empowerment
Our body
Money
Career
Spiritual growth

I have the ability to learn to clear my mind to facilitate attaining abundance I am able to get in touch with my feelings and freely express them.

I am able to get in touch with my feelings and freely express them.

I am totally honest in all of my personal and professional relationships.

I take charge of my life and remove all victimizations I encounter.

I only care for and nourish each of my physical needs.

I create abundance using the principles of karmic capitalism.

I maintain a healthy balance between my personal life and my professional goals.

I always access and listen to my Higher Self. All decisions and actions I undertake have a spiritual basis.

In order to accomplish these goals, we must obtain information that gives us a clear purpose and goal of what we desire. Next, we need to formulate a vision of this goal and eliminate any limiting beliefs that stand in the way of this abundance goal. Finally, we use affirmations, visual imagery and reprogramming techniques to both access our Higher Self and effectively reprogram the subconscious with these goals in mind.

Here is a simple exercise to assist you in establishing your karmic capitalistic goals. I highly recommend practicing the superconscious mind technique (preferably with the use of a tape) prior to answering these questions:

1. What would I do with my money if I had all that I need to take care of my needs and more?

State the spiritual principle exhibited by your answer.

2. What type of professional activity would I engage in if I was financially independent?

State the spiritual principle exhibited by your answer.

3. How would I define empowerment? Spiritual empowerment? Financial empowerment?

State the spiritual principle linking each of these definitions.

4. What specific obstacles (karmic or otherwise) have prevented me from attaining abundance? How can I overcome these obstacles?

5. State a simple abundance goal you have at this time. How may I best accomplish this goal on a win-win-win basis?

HOW TO SPECIFICALLY ATTAIN PSYCHIC EMPOWERMENT

The first question you need to ask yourself is, "How do I define power?" Some people feel power by controlling the behavior of others, such as children, spouses, employees, etc. This is a form of having power over someone, and has no spiritual basis whatsoever. It is merely a sign of insecurity.

Another way of experiencing power is by being in a certain frame of mind. Examples of this are using humor to deal with stress, being understanding or patient and being in touch with and expressing your feelings. By experiencing power as a result of your ability to both receive the energy of others and appropriately respond to it, you are demonstrating a more spiritual basis to your behavior.

Thirdly, you may very well experience power by assisting others to learn, grow and become independent. This is a true form of empowerment, and is a vital component of karmic capitalism. A balance of the last two forms of power establish a healthy balance and enables us to respond to the universe's challenges so that we may grow spiritually.

A second factor in psychic empowerment is represented by our willingness to be distracted from our vision during the trials and tribulations of life. This is commitment, and it results in confidence, fulfillment and pride in our achievements. The key to establishing commitment is having a vision that both excites and motivates you. The use of affirmations, visualizations and superconscious mind taps enables you to create a vision that you can believe in.

Discipline is required to dedicate a certain part of our day to our vision. The more compelling our vision, the easier it is to establish and maintain this vision. We always need to keep abreast as to why we are doing what we are engaged in. Commitment results from a compelling vision, and this results in discipline. Any distractions or indiscretions in our discipline can be quickly resolved by reaffirming our vision.

When I use the term Higher Self, I am specifically referring to the perfect component of our soul's energy that relates information to our conscious mind in the form of intuition, hunches and visions.

Using the superconscious mind technique involves quieting your mind and turning off the mental chatter of your rational mind. Next, you can ask your Higher Self for any information you desire. You must develop trust in this perfect component of our soul's energy. Lastly, you need to act upon these instructions to put your game plan into action to realize abundance and spiritual growth.

Love is always a component of karmic capitalism and psychic empowerment. We need to love ourselves, to love another, and to be loved by another all stimulate us to expand and open. It is in this state of loving openness that we are most capable of profound growth. Love is the most powerful motivating force in the universe. There can be no spiritual growth if love is conditional, or if you approach your goals from a perspective of pain, fear, shoulds or other obligations.

Self-love is the most important relationship we have. By validating, nurturing and accepting ourselves unconditionally, we eliminate any tendency to become codependent. This inner love is quite different than the external love that most of us consider in our definition of this term.

The superconscious mind tap and other examples of hypnosis, meditation and so on commits us to self-exploration. Love is now cultivated as you open to deeper parts of yourself, the more in touch with your true nature you get and the more you discover its essence—love. The compassion and patience we have for others, and the ability to overcome fears and negativity is represented by our inner love.

Truth is another component of psychic empowerment. When we both find our ultimate truth and live our lives based on this truth, psychic empowerment and karmic capitalism naturally result.

Society constantly tempts us to accept their truth. We are each unique and nobody else's truth will work for you. This especially applies to those "truths" espoused by bureaucracies (government, religion and corporations)—"To thine own self be true."

When you do find your ultimate truth you now possess a firm foundation to build your core beliefs and spiritual values. We now attain standards to guide us in our growth and a strong

identity as to a soul from which to function. Only you have the capability to create your own reality for life as you desire it, you must find your ultimate truth. That is what this book is all about.

In order to stimulate the spiritual development of our soul, we must remove any anger, bitterness or resentment to others. Regardless of who did what to whom, you can eliminate these hurts permanently at any time by accessing your Higher Self. Our God-given right of free will allows us to keep or discard this emotional baggage. Unfortunately, most people choose to keep them. Most of these past hurts originate from our childhood, parents, past relationships and experiences at work.

Here is a simple exercise to assist you in removing past hurts. Precede this with playing your superconscious mind tape:

1.   Visualize yourself on a long, isolated highway. This road has healing qualities at each fork in this expansive road. You may travel either back or forward in time on this road by simply using the drive or reverse gear on your car.

2.   Using the reverse gear, back up on this road to a time when you experienced a traumatic hurt in your life. Come to a healing fork in this road and communicate with the person responsible for this hurt. It may very well have been yourself at a young age who generated this self-hurt. Carry on a conversation with this individual (or yourself) and express why you were hurt.

3.   Listen to this other person and resolve this hurt now in this healing fork in the road. Pay strict attention to their truth, while immersing yourself in the healing energy at this fork in the road. Feel yourself being healed and empowered.

4.   Now place your car in the drive gear and move forward in time beyond the present to five years in the future. Arrive at a healing fork in the road and note how this hurt is long gone. See how your life has changed as a result of this cleansing, and again immerse yourself in the healing energy of this fork in the road.

HOW WE VIEW WORK

In order to become a karmic capitalist, you must love your work. This occupation should reflect your deepest concern for other people and result in somehow bettering the universe.

We tend to view our careers in five distinct ways. They may be summarized as follows:

1. A pay check. Many people look upon their job as simply a means to pay their bills. There is no passion here. A rut is established and no spiritual growth is possible now. Your feelings toward this job is neutral.

2. Dissatisfied. Your feelings toward your position is one of dislike. You may be bored, overstressed or underchallenged. The end of each workday is the only thing you look forward to.

3. Transition. This intermediary state is one in which you are between jobs, but looking forward to a new position. You are most likely searching for a new job, and probably excited about the possibilities.

4. A stepping stone. The job you currently have is simply a means to an end. Whether it's the experience, contacts or money to support you or your education, this position is only a temporary one.

5. Fulfilled. The most desirable of these five categories is doing what you truly love. This is what all karmic capitalists exhibit. When you establish a career at a position that affects your body, mind, heart and spirit you will be fulfilled and satisfied.

AN EXERCISE TO CREATE YOUR IDEAL CAREER

It is critical for you to create a vision for your work that represents what you would most love to do. This exercise consists of posing certain questions to your Higher Self to assist you creating your vision of karmic capitalism. Just think of what your life would be like if all of your creativity, talents, uniqueness and passions were engaged in your work. By integrating your body, mind and soul with your highest personal and professional values in your chosen career, you can make great strides to becoming a karmic capitalist.

Always remember that the way to make money is to do exactly what you want to do and do it exactly the way you want to do it. The principal way to achieve wealth is to stay as closely as possible to your own inner vision. Only your own idea can fuel you with the energy and passion to continue during the inevitable early discouragements. Your Higher Self will always be there helping you along the way.

Precede this exercise by playing your superconscious mind tape:

1.   Create an ideal environment for your work. Focus on as many details as you can in this setting. List the office, outdoor facilities, the style of the building, equipment, computers, home-office and so on.

2.   Now focus on your exact duties and write a brief summary of your daily activities. If you are involved with creative projects, list some of your past achievements and current assignments.

3.   See how you relate to others in your work environment. Do you work alone, or have many people around you? How long is your workday? Describe the level of formality in this setting. Is this your own business, or are you an employee?

4.   Describe your values, ideals and goals in your occupation. Focus in on your level of commitment, integrity, compassion and spirituality. Rate the importance of each.

5.   Write a brief summary of the talents and innovations you exhibit in this ideal vocation. Focus also on challenges, pet projects and interests that allow you to maximize your creative talents.

6.   Describe your coworkers and employees and the relationship you have with them. Include in this the structure of this company, with special emphasis on any characteristics of corporate karmic capitalism.

7.   Relate any professional recognition you receive for your work. Reference involvement with the community, environmental groups and public communication.

8.   Complete this overview of your ideal creative and work vision by listing your income, net worth and anything else that is characteristic of this life professional vision.

Now concentrate on this vision and allow your Higher Self to assist you in making this a part of your reality. Experience the bliss of this vision in your heart, mind and body. Recognize that by concentrating on this image and accepting the belief that you have the power to create this vision, it will become your destiny.

This blueprint you have just created may have been a completely different vocation than you have presently. It may have been simply an extension of your current work. Have faith and trust in your Higher Self to facilitate your natural ability to realize this ideal.

WHAT DOES SPIRITUALITY MEAN TO ME?

I cannot discuss karmic capitalism without emphasizing the spiritual growth component of this paradigm. Spirituality is all around us in the love, compassion, kindness, generosity, trust, sensitivity, integrity and wisdom in the universe. We have other gifts, such as creative abilities and healing powers that demonstrate it is our responsibility to use these gifts to the fullest to make the universe a better place.

The only person responsible and in control of your own spiritual unfoldment is you. As we grow in spirituality, a gift takes places from a dependent relationship to merging with our Higher Self (the white light) and functioning as a co-creator with God in the universe. This eliminates all tendencies to being a victim of circumstances.

You are a creative force in the universe. Each and every day you are co-crating the world through what you believe and the actions you take. An advanced form of psychic empowerment is exhibited when you direct your actions to helping others and improving the universe.

A continual alignment of your actions with the karmic purpose you selected prior to this earthly incarnation is required to keep you on this spiritual path. Every decision you make should be a spiritual one. It should always affirmatively answer the question, "Will this action or decision align me with my Higher Self and add to the quality of the universe?"

The higher purpose you selected has nothing to do with the do's and don't's of religion or society. It has everything to do with your soul's purpose and spiritual unfoldment.

Do not confuse spirituality with the doctrine and dogma of religion. Our spirituality is quite personal, differs from that of everyone else and represents a personal and intimate contact with our Higher Self. This spiritual path is your ultimate truth and reflects the deepest aspects of our soul and very being.

Since spirituality is individually unique, your spiritual lessons are not better or worse than anyone else's—they are simply different. We create our spiritual paths to learn karmic lessons. Each of us must create his or her own spiritual path. As we integrate our ultimate truth into our world view, we move from accepting others into encouraging them to find their own paths. We each need to move toward fulfilling our unique higher purpose to grow spiritually.

The spiritual reason for us being on this planet is related to specific lessons we have to learn. These lessons are easiest to master when we align ourselves with our true inner nature, our Higher Self. This is the main reason I emphasize the superconscious mind exercise. Any profound experience we have is but an example of this Higher Self communicating with us directly and demonstrating its presence.

Here is an exercise that will assist you in aligning yourself with your Higher Self and reflect upon transcendental experiences you have had. Precede this series of instructions with the playing of your superconscious mind tape.

1.   Review your subconscious memory banks with the assistance of your Higher Self, and specifically focus on moving or memorable encounters that transcended your normal state of mind.

2.   Now recall a past event that literally changed the direction of your life. This event does not have to be a professional one. It is more important that it reflect a spiritual awakening. Re-experience this profound incident from the depths of your soul, as if it were occurring now.

3.   Request your Higher Self inform you of one important element of your spiritual path that you are currently working on. This is an aspect of your karmic purpose, and one that will assist you with an immediate issue resulting in spiritual growth.

ELIMINATING BELIEFS THAT BLOCK SPIRITUAL GROWTH

Here are some typical limiting beliefs concerning spirituality and abundance, along with new beliefs that assist with your spiritual unfoldment.

Limiting Belief: I have to sacrifice my spiritual growth if I am going to attain abundance.

New Belief: The universe is designed to foster both peace, harmony, beauty, love kindness, joy and other aspects of spirituality along with abundance. It doesn't matter how much money I have, all that matters is how I acquire it and the manner in which I preserve it.

Limiting Belief: The earth plane is, and always will be, characterized by suffering.

New Belief: I create my universe. If I choose to fill it with love, play, joy, harmony, and oneness, then in time these characteristics will dominate the planet.

Limiting Belief: I have to give up control over my life to a higher power outside of me to grow spiritually.

New Belief: My Higher Self is within me and a component of the God energy complex.

I alone direct and control my life through my thoughts and actions, while maintaining a connection with my Higher Self.

CHAPTER 8

CORPORATE KARMIC CAPITALISM

In A Study of History, The British historian Arnold Toynbee spoke of the possible "transfiguration" of modern society into some kind of respiritualized form. The industrial revolution promised a better life for all Americans. It most certainly delivered this promise——but at a tremendous cost to its citizens. As long as people needed more and more material possessions, this paradigm worked.

Such thirst for a higher "standard of living" regardless of moral, ethical, emotional, cultural, spiritual, marital, environmental and political consequences pervaded the American scene, and still does. Corporate America provided transportation in the form of railroads, cars and airplanes. Agriculture was mechanized to feed our people. Cheap energy and labor-saving devices freed up human energy, mass communication was established so that we could stay in touch with one another from "sea to shining sea."

During the latter half of the twentieth century things began to change. Material possessions now transformed themselves from fulfilling basic needs to enhancing luxuries. Excesses became the norm. We went from individual national economies to an increasingly global economy. Still, our obsession was to keep up with the Joneses. Unlike in the past, problems began to emerge that could not be solved by providing more material goods. Not only that, but these problems were not restricted to Western industrialized nations but became global in nature.

This affected our entire planet, as water shortages, topsoil loss, global warming, ozone holes, species extinction, natural resource degradation and depletion, air pollution and trash buildup made our daily headlines. We may have won the Industrial Revolution, but we most certainly are losing the peace that followed. The old road map for money has us trapped in the very vehicle that was supposed to liberate us from toil. This old road map is no longer guiding us to the American Dream.

For example, The Wall Street Journal reported in 1991 that:
• The average North American works 20 percent more today than in 1973 and has 32 percent less free time per week.
• 48 percent of 4,126 male executives saw their lives as "empty and meaningless" despite years of professional striving.
• "90 percent of all divorces are caused by money," according to financial planner and psychologist Victoria Felton-Collins.
• The divorce rate is 34 percent higher than in 1970.
• The life savings of the average 50-year-old is $2,300.
• The number of American children living below the poverty line has increased from 14.9 percent in 1970 to 19 percent in 1990.
• 31 percent of those surveyed worry that they don't spend enough time with their families and friends, and 38 percent say they are cutting back on sleep to make more time (to earn more money).
• Personal bankruptcies have been climbing steeply since the 1950s.
• The number of individuals spending more than they earn has increased greatly among those whose income is in the lower fortieth percentile.

In his book The Transformations of Man, Lewis Mumford described about six previous transformations of Western civilization. He went on to predict a coming transformation that would be obvious only to a very few contemporary observers:

"Every [human] transformation...has rested on a new metaphysical and ideological base; or rather, upon deeper stirrings and intuitions whose rationalized expression takes the form of a new picture of the cosmos and the nature of man.... We stand on the brink of [such] a new age: the age of an open world and of a self capable of playing its part in that larger sphere. An age of renewal, when work and leisure and learning and love will unite to produce a fresh form for every stage of life, and a higher trajectory for life as a whole....In carrying[human]...self-transformation to this further stage, world culture may bring about a fresh release of spiritual energy that will unveil new potentialities, no more visible in the human self today than radium was in the physical world a century ago, though always present....Who can set bounds to man's emergence or to his power of surpassing his provisional achievements? So far we have found no limits to the imagination, nor yet to the sources on which it may draw. Every goal [humanity]...reaches provides a new starting point, and the sum of all [humanity's]...days is just beginning."

Although society continually exhibits change, Mumford's thesis emphasizes that there are certain periods of history when these changes are more fundamental and involve all institutions and basic components of culture. The most recent transformation occurred at the end of the Middle Ages.

These changes relate to the dominant paradigms of our culture and express themselves in the basic ways of perceiving, thinking, valuing, and actions associated with a particular view of reality. Alterations of the very fabric of society that characterize it and underlie its very foundations are evident during this transformation. A paradigm shift is not taught per se, but naturally adopted by each member of society. These alterations are not critically evaluated, but are accepted as true and factual.

Contemporary authorities have arrived at similar conclusions concerning this current transformation. For example, we see this paradigm presented in:

- Marilyn Ferguson's The Aquarian Conspiracy
- Alvin Toffler's The Third Wave
- Fritj of Capra's The Turning Point

Alvin Toffler clearly alluded to this transformation when he averred:

"Despite what today's parties and candidates may preach, the infighting among them amounts to little more than a dispute over who will squeeze the most advantage from what remains of the declining industrial system....While short-range political skirmishes exhaust our energy and attention, a far more profound battle is already taking place beneath the surface. On one side are the partisans of the industrial past; on the other, growing millions who recognize that the most urgent problems of the world——food, energy, arms control, population, poverty, resources, ecology, climate, the problems of the aged, the breakdown of urban community, the need for productive, rewarding work——can no longer be resolved within the framework of the industrial order."

Since our world today is more tightly interconnected as a result of advances in communication technology, these changes are occurring at a faster rate and are becoming evident now. Corporations are beginning to address global issues of poverty, environment, and security. They are also turning to techniques developed by brain researchers that release employees' barriers to creativity and intuition. Taking place now is a global application of the principle that by deliberately changing their internal image of reality, people change the world.

There are four main theories of employee motivation and work organization. These can be listed as: (a) meritocracy, (b) egalitarianism, (c)

139

behaviorism and (d) humanism. Meritocracy advocates believe that there are real, fundamental differences in individual talents, abilities, and willingness to work, and that these differences should be acknowledged and rewarded accordingly. Bonuses should be presented to those employees who are most productive, while people who consistently perform poorly should be let go. Libertarian and other market-oriented economists tend to support meritocratic forms of organization.

Those who feel that employees are to be protected by "entitlements," should be paid equally for equal work and have guaranteed job security favor the egalitarian theory. This form of work approach is supported by socialist economists and trade unionists.

Behaviorists follow the model that human behavior is a response to environmental conditioning, employee performance is closely monitored and regulated and elaborate incentive schemes should reward efficient and productive behavior. Finally, the humanists present the approach that the true purpose of work is to extract full potential from the employee. This theory emphasizes a key role in decision making by the employee. In addition, organizational policies and practices should be designed to enhance personal growth and development.

Corporate karmic capitalists apply all four of these theories in the workplace. There is no one proper paradigm or sequential order or percentage of these paradigms. Each company adopts these approaches in a manner that reflects its own particular size, industry, melting pot of employees and managers, environment and other factors.

CHANGING CONSCIOUSNESS

The global aspect of commerce today has resulted in the beginning of an emerging vision of a new and positive future for our planet. This transformation is not as yet fully apparent, but it most certainly involves reassessment of the scientific understanding of the human mind and spirit; of our ecological relationship to the planet; of the assurance of peace and common security; and of the role of business in creating a meaningful and viable future.

Business has finally begun to accept the fact that only through a change in the basic paradigm can we possibly resolve the various issues and global dilemmas we face at present. The old beliefs are now being questioned and systematically discarded. For instance, consider these examples of the old paradigm:

- Primitive cultures need to be modernized.
- Women can have only subordinate roles in society.
- The Earth exists to be exploited.
- Nonwhite people are inferior.
- Perpetual increases in consumption are always good for the economy.
- Nuclear weapons result in "national security."

We must never forget the basis of capitalism and democracy: All institutions in society obtain their legitimacy from the perceptions of people, and that people have the power to change institutions and discard them by challenging the legitimacy. Perhaps only 5 to 10 percent of the adult population in America is aware of this transformation today. Research in current values has shown that as many as 50 percent of Americans in the 1990s espouse values significantly different from those characteristic of the explosive economic growth of the 1950s and early 1960s. Similar changes are evident in northern Europe, Canada, Australia, and to a lesser extent in the Eastern European countries and Third World nations.

The current transformation of the corporate world has five components: search for community and relationship, search for identity, search for meaning, search for wholeness, and sense of empowerment.

1. Search for community and relationship. A depersonalization, an alienation, has been brought about by most jobs located away from home. To counter this, a rise has been noted in corporate-sponsored group therapies, human relations workshops and similar programs encouraging others to relate more deeply with their fellow citizens. Businesses have organized retreats to "get back to nature."

Technologies are being developed to enhance instead of diminish our human nature. Holistic health care stressing prevention, organic agriculture focusing on replenishing the soil with natural methods of pest control and renewable resource energy practices are but a few examples of this principle.

2. Search for identity. Weekend workshops and other experiential forms of psychotherapy abound today and act in diametric opposite directions to the "Me Generation" approach of the 1970s and 1980s. Two of the largest traditionally oppressed groups in society, women and the Third World nations, have rebelled against the paradigms since the 1960s.

The women's movement has emphasized more cooperative and nurturing values, while the Third World groups have stressed alternative forms of economic development more compatible with their cultural roots.

3.   Search for meaning. A vacuum in the meaning of life has surfaced following the reductionist scientific debunking of religion, and the lack of fulfillment from mere technological advancement by science. We see an increased interest in Eastern philosophy and theology to compensate for the inability of Western science to adequately explain the entire spectrum of the human experience.

Massive exploration of altered states of consciousness through hypnosis, yoga, meditation and psychedelic drugs (unfortunately) has abounded since the 1960s. This attempt at inner exploration of the mind (consciousness) has been characterized by self-realization, transcendental meanings, and inner growth with an attempt to foster wisdom and compassion. We can see a UP-3 paradigm spreading rapidly in the West.

4.   Search for wholeness. The world has been characterized by the fragmentation and separation of one's job, religion, recreational time, and so on from the rest of life. Movements such as holistic health, Green political parties and others have reintroduced a sense of wholeness into society.

Corporations now provide in-house day care, employee assistance programs for psychological problems, and other avenues to attempt to bridge this gap. It is only through a holistic approach, uniting body, mind and spirit, that these issues will eventually be resolved.

We can look to "deep ecology" paradigms moving well beyond conventional scientific UP-1 approaches, to an awareness of the oneness of all life and a multiple-interconnectedness of the planetary ecosystem to foster this transformation so long overdue.

5.   Sense of empowerment. It is refreshing to observe the extent to which people are awakening and feeling empowered to take responsibility for their own lives and for changing society. Corporations too exemplify this concept and are probably the most adaptive institution humankind has ever devised. Business journals such as Business Month and Harvard Business Review have begun to publish articles referring to the use of hunches and intuition in business decision making. Management development courses in recent years have been steadily open about recommending imagery and affirmation approaches to develop both intuition and creativity. Classic studies illustrate that successful people visualize their goals and use affirmations to reinforce their confidence in making these goals a reality.

We are seeing with greater frequency management styles based on the paradigm that people are fundamentally honest, purposeful and good. This is the reverse of the previous mentality of big business.

KARMIC CAPITALISM PRINCIPLES
BEING EXHIBITED TODAY

In the next chapter I will present examples of corporate karmic capitalism in large businesses. The following examples of general business trends noted today begin to demonstrate a transformation in the business world toward karmic capitalism:

1.   The tendency to allow employees the opportunities to do what they do best. By ascertaining the main interests and talents of employees, management has discovered that this builds on people's strength and improves productivity.

2.   Assigning tasks that stimulate personal and professional growth works in conjunction with the principle in the preceding paragraph.

3.   Promoting personnel on merit, rather than the traditional seniority system, fosters self-respect and enthusiasm on the job.

4.   Maintaining an atmosphere that shows it is safe to make an error eliminates the fear-provoking effect, and decreases deception and creative blocks.

5.   Keeping an open mind to opposing points of view conveys respect for the employee. This is contrary to the previous trend of punishing dissent so commonly exhibited by old paradigms.

6.   Inviting an employee who has performed beyond expectations to explore with others how this came about assists in raising their consciousness and serves as a model for others to do the same.

7.   Presenting an atmosphere of being interested in solutions, not blaming, further promotes self-esteem and creativity.

8.   The key personnel who set standards of personal integrity by keeping their promises and honoring their commitments establish healthier role models for employees and generate pride in working for such a moral organization.

9.   The growing tendency for management taking personal responsibility for creating a work environment promoting self-esteem, ethics and creativity further enhances karmic capitalism. Great managers are not the ones who come up with truly innovative ideas, but stimulate their staff to initiate brilliant solutions.

We can look to Perry Pascarella who in his book The New Achievers writes:

"A quiet revolution is taking place...in the business corporation....Although we have been hearing more and more about corporate efforts in human resource development in recent years, we may miss the essential truth about what is happening: Individuals are awakening to the possibility of personal growth and finding opportunities to attain it. The team building we hear about is secondary to the development of the individual....Management is heading toward a new state of mind——a new perception of its own role and that of the organization. It is slowly moving from seeking power to empowering others, from controlling people to enabling them to be creative....As managers make a fundamental ship in values...the corporation [undergoes] a radical reorientation to a greater worldview."

We can see from these examples that the movement to create an internal work environment that fosters personal growth and creativity is emerging. These organizations have a strong sense of corporate vision that has been communally developed, and a strong focus around that vision.

The global aspect of business today transcends national boundaries. It is not just economies, but societies themselves that are affected by corporate decisions. Up until the present there has been no adequate guiding ethic. Karmic capitalist tendencies now make it critical that spiritual codes of ethics be instituted to truly complete this transformation.

A new form of thinking is required in which jobs exist primarily for self-development, and is only secondarily concerned with the production of goods and services. It is only through a UP-3 paradigm that such a radical concept could be initiated. We can look to the ancient Greek concept of paideia as a model.

The Greek term paideia referred to a lifelong transformation of the individual in which education was the key to linking all aspects of life together in this learning process. The Greek "learning society's" primary function was to promote learning at all levels. The attainment of wholeness, not merely the conscious learning process, took precedence over any other activity.

To apply paideia in modern business, we need to promote a diversity of activities, such as self-discovery, creativity, community involvement, education, fine arts, athletics, research and consciousness expansion. Anything that contributes to the fulfillment of workers and the betterment of humankind fits in with this form of karmic capitalism.

Businesses on the leading edge of transformation and karmic capitalism always concern themselves with meaning. Traditionally, businesses have fostered a disintegration of meaning to individual workers and this has resulted in the creation of marginal people——people who live at the margins of society and have no real place, whether unemployed, underemployed, or unemployable. To more competently encourage growth with this marginal population, a "developing society" must be established. This paradigm promotes the maximum potential for each individual. Some of the examples I present in chapter 9 illustrate this developing society principle.

Corporations exhibiting karmic capitalism recognize the fact that the employee's desire to produce and create must originate internally, and not from external pressures. This arises from the person's consciousness of his or her relationship to the whole rather than from fear tactics or a desire for the approval of others.

From this discussion we can see a growing trend in large corporations to create a work environment that fosters the individual's actualizing his or her own latent creativity, and on evolving highly autonomous business units in which local initiative and control can operate to the fullest extent possible. Some examples of this new management style include:

- A structure characterized by decentralization and flexibility.
- An environment that emphasizes growth and empowerment of the individual.
- A coagulation of members of the company on all levels to a shared vision.
- A shared sense of personal responsibility for business goals.
- A deep sense of purposefulness and a shared vision of the future.

LEARNING FROM PAST MISTAKES

Progressive businesses today have learned from the mistakes of the past. To fully comprehend the new creative force of corporate karmic capitalists, let us review what simply didn't work:

In the past a poverty-stricken mind-set dominated business. This paradigm was characterized by a persistent fear of never having enough. The possibility that people's hopes might be deceptive created an opposing force of fear. This fear, in turn, initiated an insecurity mechanism whereby the world was divided into "good" and "bad" or "us" versus "them."

Although this division may have produced a temporary feeling of security, problems surfaced in the form of isolation, disillusionment and constraints. By attempting to shape both people and the environment to fit this distorted concept, the very richness and meaning of life was blocked, resulting in a craving for power, love, prestige and security.

This addiction to security and prestige led to hypocritical behavior and subsequent fault-seeking from subordinates. The result of this pattern naturally caused the prevention of learning from mistakes and generated an environment in which employees were unwilling to take risks. As a consequence creativity was stifled, morale was destroyed, and none of these factors could now be solved by more money or more free time.

The corporate examples of karmic capitalism quickly adopted the paradigm of encouraging open awareness and creativity. By trusting the whole person, these businesses do not rely on their conscious mind alone, but include their subconscious in decision making and planning. They learned to function beyond value judgment and thereby eliminated many previous restrictions to spiritual growth.

Now business is more than making money. Business is combined with art, metaphysics and spirituality functioning as a unit, which stimulates the whole person to maximize his or her creativity. This quantum leap in consciousness requires businesses to look beyond the opposing forces of fear and hope to creative, not conventional, solutions that represent a commitment to integrity and accountability for the well-being of many.

We must never underestimate the effect business, with its associated technological capabilities, as a powerful shaping force of the future. Since the corporate world creates most of the jobs in society and attracts its most creative people, is it so surprising that this organization form is on the cutting edge of a transformation?

Modern industry is steadily moving toward the creation of a work environment that promotes creative initiative and meaningful participation. Competition now acts to attract and hold the very best people, who will be enticed by the improving quality of the work environment.

A spontaneous awakening is taking place in corporate karmic capitalism. Personal development seminars and courses offered by these progressive companies are focused on awareness and cultivation of personal empowerment. They foster the concept that employees can create whatever they choose to. Another philosophy promoted by these educational opportunities is the discovery of one's Higher Self in the form of inner wisdom that both guides creative choices and contribute to its accomplishment.

The main theme of these forms of karmic continuing education is that everything is connected to everything else, and that no one really wins unless all do. Techniques of affirmation and visualization further accentuate this paradigm. Awareness of the expanded nature of these inner resources leads to a shift in the individual's perceived source of authority, away from external dogmas and "experts" of all kinds, and toward deepened trust in the inner, intuitive authority of one's Higher Self.

Management now functions to encourage others to develop and use their natural creative gifts. A sense of self-empowerment and inner guidance permeates the entire company. Our society will be shaped more by business than government, since business has become the predominant institution in the modern world.

The traditional motivators for job performance——job security, high pay, and good benefits——no longer work. Employees now want work that is personally satisfying, offers ample opportunity to learn new skills and to grow personally, presents a reasonable amount of autonomy, and allows recognition for good work. The fact that work should be both economically rewarding and emotionally fulfilling has been confirmed by studies reported by Naisbitt and Maccoby.

Naisbitt states that corporate America is coming to a new "ideal of the model employee....We are shifting the ideal...from one who carries out orders correctly to one who takes responsibility and initiative, monitors his or her own work, and uses managers and supervisors in their new roles as facilitators, teachers, and consultants."

This radical notion that workers can manage themselves parallels demands for rights of participation commensurate with their responsibilities. Another empowerment trend is that of workers-owned organizations, from the Employee Stock Option Plans (ESOP) in which the workers become part owners by virtue of acquiring stock in the company, to the workers-owned-and-managed Mondragon cooperatives in the Basque region of Spain. As relationships become more important than materialistic concerns, as wholeness and oneness replace separateness and competition, the way is opened for a new, more cooperative and familial kind of organization to become the norm.

We see a global economy today: research, design, fabrication, assembly, and marketing are now a global operation. Issues that might once have been the concerns of individual companies now have global significance. Everything is connected to everything else. Economic decisions and policies cannot be made solely on the basis of optimizing some economic parameters without taking into account politics, social situations, value considerations, and ecological realities.

Competition in economic systems has the same effect as competition in ecosystems: It reduces the number of competitors. In ecosystems, adaptive changes come not from the species dominant in their niche, but from species and individuals existing on the fringe and forced to be more resourceful. We can thus expect women, minorities and small entrepreneurial companies to initiate the transformations I have been describing.

Most current businesses are characterized by waste, competition and growth by overconsumption. This model is unstable and will eventually result in a declining standard of living. This has also brought to the forefront a crisis of meaning and values.

There has developed a total absence of consensus in the area of basic values and central meaning. The drive for meaning is the strongest of all value drives. A renewed search for spiritual values has surfaced, as I previously described. Its most important aspects are 1) the shift from seeking the "right" external authority to a focus on discovering the source of inner wisdom; and 2) the quiet infusion of the "new meaning" into all forms of business and professional life.

The transformation has already begun, and is fueled by: 1) an emphasis on wholeness, unity, interconnectedness; and 2) an emphasis on inner authority, integrity, discovering inner knowing and wisdom, drawing on hidden inner resources. No one is left behind in this process. Every person plays a pivotal role in the transformation of society, since we are all connected by our Higher Selves to a global consciousness.

Since the workplace has become the central institution of society, largely replacing the family, the place of worship, and the community, the company (or employer) is often in the best position to become the "source of inspiration and purpose" in the life of the working person. It is no longer enough to "have a job" or even a "career." Such people are looking for deeper meaning in their lives. Past measures of success such as material gain, status, or positions no longer satisfy a fulfillment need that many are experiencing. These people are increasingly concerned about a deeper sense of life purpose.

Marsha Sinetar also emphasizes the importance of personal growth in the future. She writes:

"A key management issue of the year 2000 will be these workers' increasing need for self-actualization. By actualization I mean a healthy personality, wholeness, a full-functioning being, and psychological 'completion.' The self-actualized person is creative, independent, and self-sufficient. These individuals will increasingly have as their primary focus personal goals, inner values, and the creation of distinct lifestyles."

Social transcendence and self-transcendence are noted by Sinetar as qualities appearing more frequently today. Both of these traits are critical to self-actualization. An individual's achievement of emotional independence from societal influences, including those of authority figures, family, co-workers, and other previously significant persons, is what the term social transcendence means.

The confident, independent and creative worker who seeks to merge inner truths and values with outer realities, hoping to embody——in daily life and through a life's work——the light, ideals, and unique talent found within, is the most sought-after employee of corporate karmic capitalists today. These valued workers strive to incorporate whatever work they do into a meaningful and fulfilling life context——one that is both inwardly rewarding and outwardly creative.

We already see how small companies are taking the lead in the transformation process. These fast, agile companies that thrive on change are the perfect model for this major shift. Paul Hawken states: "Since 1973, the Fortune 500 companies have lost a net of 6,000,000 jobs, passed off as part of becoming 'lean and mean,' of slimming down, restructuring, and competitiveness——terms that ring hollow to the men and women who were its victims. During this same period, however, 23,000,000 net new jobs were created in the U.S. and 98 percent of them came from businesses with 100 employees or less."

David Birch also echoes these sentiments when he writes: "...there is no such thing as an American economy, at least not in the way the term is usually employed. Rather, there are about 7 million companies, close to 90 percent of which employ fewer than 20 workers. Taken together these small companies create more jobs than the Fortune 500, grow more rapidly, run greater chances of failure, and show more adaptability."

David Birch, author of Job Creation in America, notes that when this transformation is complete, one main feature of corporate karmic capitalistic businesses will be a devolution of power to the local level——ultimately, to within the individual. Here are some characteristics and goals that we are already seeing by leading-edge corporate karmic capitalists:

• A commitment throughout each decade to leave the major ecological and life-support systems of the planet in at least as good shape as the decade before.

• Emphasis on a socially constructive role for business, beyond the economic.

- Focus on self-help and the development of new individual ways of being.
- Decentralization of power from higher to lower levels.
- De-bureaucratization.
- Balance of economic and spiritual growth objectives.
- Emphasis on work as vocation, as a central and fulfilling aspect of one's life.
- Resurgence of localism.
- Worker self-management and humanization of the workplace.
- Return to human scale in structuring.

We can look to small companies to take the lead in the transformation to corporate karmic capitalism for the simple reason that they are created to change our culture and to solve problems that cannot be solved by money alone.

Simplicity has always been the answer to corporate success. Employees need to be self-confident and empowered to be productive. Most global companies have only three or four competitors, and these are well known. Small businesses respond more rapidly to market changes. They are often the ones to come up with new ideas and new values.

To effect this corporate transformation, the individual employee must undergo a radical change as well. An entirely new way of thinking and functioning will be required. Many executives may have difficulty in adjusting to this paradigm, and may need to reevaluate their own self-image and level of competence.

These corporate karmic capitalists create very democratic work environments that require a high degree of accountability and responsible participation by all its employees. In reality, there is no such thing as a corporate transformation, there is only individual transformation. As change continues to become a more significant part of corporate life, it will be increasingly important to learn how to respond and recover from major change——both organizationally and personally. By understanding the dynamics of the change process, individuals and employees will have more energy to focus on the growth opportunities that change offers, rather than on the resistance that is naturally associated with this change.

In the past 25 years or so, this change has resulted in escalating competition, limited resources, and changes in attitude about work, male-female roles, and management styles. We can define the culture of a corporation as that system of interrelated, standardized, institutionalized and habitual behavior that is characteristic of a particular company.

Any attempt at change, which all corporate karmic capitalists must continually enact, must deal with deep levels of this culture. Merely altering the management style or company logo will fail to bring about a permanent or significant transformation.

The new management style of corporate karmic capitalists will consist of:

- Profit sharing and employee ownership.
- Autonomous and relatively small business units.
- Few levels of management.
- Encouraging shared visions.
- Learning how to learn.
- Planning and leading by example.

These policies must be instituted immediately. The company that simply waits for the various methods of transformation to be proven effective before enacting them will not be around to initiate an attempt at this paradigm.

We see examples of more subtle and "softer" areas of this transformation. Some of these are alignment of purpose, respect for the individual, steadfastness, coaching, relationships, patience, participative processes, stress management, involvement of spouse and families and community support. It must be remembered that the managers in these forward-thinking companies were inspired by the visions of the 1960s and 1970s, and are now in a position to make them a reality. Since the global culture is in a change phase, we are beginning to see it manifested in these companies.

Roger Harrison writes in an article titled "Strategies for a New Age": "Purpose and intention are far more powerful than plans. Never in my years as a consultant have I seen an organization changed in any fundamental way through rational planning. The leaders I have seen deeply influence their organization's characters and destinies have always operated out of intuition, guided by strongly held purposes and drawn on by a vision of a better future. They communicated their intentions verbally to others who could share their vision, and they communicated it daily to others through their 'real time' actions and decisions. In due course, enough people shared the vision and the intention to reach 'critical mass,' and the dream became reality."

We Americans have become increasingly cynical and disenchanted with the business establishment while we overwhelmingly support the capitalistic system of free enterprise; a belief that corporations operate almost exclusively for the benefit of management and stockholders permeates through the culture. These same people surveyed insist that corporations should function for the benefit of employees, customers, and society in general.

This public mistrust of corporations can be altered only through changes in the very behavior that produced this suspicion. By dealing openly and with the highest integrity with employees, shareholders, customers, and society as a whole, this aura will be altered to one of win-win-win. To be true karmic capitalists, corporations need to establish standards of excellence in all phases of operation——such as truth in advertising, quality of products, accuracy of labeling, appropriate disclosure, job content, working conditions, and upward mobility for women and minorities.

Corporate karmic capitalists must train their top management people to consistently communicate visions and policies reflecting noble aspirations and purpose. Great corporations are governed by great ideas, and karmically capitalistic companies are run with a spiritual growth mentality.

An openness to rethink the very basis of the company itself is also required. The upper management needs to at times unlearn the old ways of doing business even though those methods may have been successful in producing large profits. This openness to learning is one of the most significant differences between corporate karmic capitalists and the old-thought businesses.

University of Southern California management professor James O'Toole states in his book Vanguard Management that "vanguard" corporations exhibit "commitment in word and deed to a higher purpose: These corporations exist to provide society with the goods and services it needs, to provide employment, and to create a surplus of wealth (profit) with which to improve the nation's general standard of living and quality of life. In this view, profit is the means, not the end of corporate activity."

We can look to Robert Levering, co-author of The 100 Best Companies to Work for in America for additional insights into karmic capitalism on the corporate level:

"Employees at 'good workplaces' often remark that the company gives them a lot of responsibility. Those who have worked elsewhere often suggest that the biggest change they notice is the greater level of responsibility they are given....Responsibility implies control. The issue of control strikes at the very core of what distinguishes good workplaces....When people report that they have responsibility and control over their work, they mean that they have some power...a role in defining their own jobs——determining priorities and deadlines, and determining actions taken by others (including supervisors and top management) without fear of retribution."

Just as a futurist living during the Renaissance would find it next to impossible to describe society today, so is it difficult for the old-thought businessperson to envision society only a few generations from now. We will see in the next chapter just how leading-edge corporate karmic capitalists and small entrepreneurs are demonstrating an application of the UP-3 paradigm, and the fact that a global transformation is underway.

CHAPTER 9

EXAMPLES OF CORPORATE KARMIC CAPITALISM

FEL-PRO

We can look to a company that manufactures sealants and engine gaskets in Skokie, Illinois named Fel-Pro for a corporate application of karmic capitalistic principles. Despite its heavy dependence on the auto industry, with its cyclical layoffs, Fel-Pro has never initiated a group layoff. During its lean times this compassionate company builds their inventories, places its employees in less paying positions without decreasing their salaries, and cuts back work schedules to a four-day work week only during the toughest times.

Fel-Pro owns a wooded 200-acre facility in Cary, Illinois, with lakes for fishing, an olympic-size swimming pool and picnic facilities. Their workers can send their children to a day camp there for a nominal fee (which includes all of their children, irrespective of the number), and invite as many as nine guests to this retreat.

Lawyers, income-tax preparers and counselors are present there, who provide free assistance to these workers. A portion of the diagnostic testing of children of these workers with learning problems is paid for by Fel-Pro. Lastly, to illustrate their commitment to the community, employees involved in community organizations can ask for donations on the group's behalf. Requests are reviewed by a committee, and Fel-Pro often makes sizable donations to these groups.

GORE

W. L. Gore & Association (Gore), based in Newark, Delaware, has initiated a rather interesting system of management and organization that they term The Lattice System since the 1960s. Gore's main product is a synthetic fiber, Gore-Tex, that is used in many electronic, medical and industrial products.

This family-held plastics corporation was started by Bill Gore, who was a research chemist with Du Pont for seventeen years. The Lattice System he designed instituted an approach to nonmanagement. This paradigm establishes and encourages direct person-to-person contact and a form of self-commitment and responsibility.

There are no fixed hierarchies Instead, Gore functions on four principles that can be summarized as follows:

1.   Commitment. Total and free commitment is encouraged by the absence of authoritarian hierarchies.

2.   Fairness. Cooperation and communication is a significant component to the Gore philosophy.

3.*   Waterline. Before any significant risks are undertaken, consultations with experts outside of the company are sought.

4.   Freedom. Complete freedom of expression is fostered to promote creativity and innovative ideas.

* The expression "drilling holes under the waterline" is applied to risky decisions in business vernacular.

Gore has experienced an explosive development as a result of applying this nonmanagerial approach.   Bill Gore began this enterprise in the basement of his home. By 1992 Gore had plants in the U.S., Scotland, Japan, France and Germany. Over 5,000 employees comprise this company, and its annual sales are more than 700 million dollars. It is considered one of the top five percent of U.S. companies in relation to return on assets and equity. An interesting philosophy of Gore is to keep the total employees in a factory to less than 200. Another factory is constructed when this number is approached.

WILSON LEARNING CORPORATION

The Wilson Learning Corporation was founded by Larry Wilson, and this company specializes in the sales of courses in administration, management, sales and leadership. This corporate karmic capitalist's clients are progressive management executives from large corporations.

These top executives are being trained to master the principles of corporate karmic capitalism that reflect the leading edge of our culture. The UP-3 paradigms represented by this New Mexico corporation can be described by the following four "learnings" taught at this establishment.

1.   Creating a vision. The Wilson Learning Corporation does not teach pressuring oneself for a vision, but actualizing it with an alignment with the individual's sense of purpose into a collective vision with the rest of the organization. What many might interpret as "luck breaks," "coincidences" or just "hunches" are internal mechanisms of realizing this sense of purpose.

2.   Purpose. The reason for being on the Earth in the first is one component of our purpose. A limitless source of motivation results when an organization is built around the goal of assisting each individual worker to self-actualize and function from that deep sense of purpose.

In order to align oneself with this deep inner purpose (karmic purpose), we must have no other goals. This Eastern form of philosophy applied to Western business implies an elimination from our mind set during this process all other ambitions, ideals, predilections, hopes, desires, plans and rational thought. Both visual imagery and affirmations may be used to bring this about.

3.   Fears and Trust. Both fear and trust are choices made subconsciously. Experiential exercises are designed to both illustrate and overcome these obstacles to growth. Scaling a cliff with the aid of a safety harness can be applied with fear issues. Trust is established by assigning projects that require the feedback and participation of others to complete.

One interesting example of the latter principle was establishing a goal of scaling an eighteen foot wall without any equipment or other aids. The only solution possible was to form a human pyramid!

Affirmations are used to remove fear and establish trust. For example, the following affirmations were proposed:

- I can trust others.
- I can trust myself.
- There is nothing to fear in the world.
- I need not be anxious about tomorrow, as the universe will always provide the basis for me to solve any problem.

To utilize affirmations properly is to program the subconscious to view the world as being different than that accepted by the go.

4.   Acting with feedback. Everything we encounter in our universe is to be thought of as feedback, not good or bad. The inner decision to follow our deep sense of purpose is far more significant than whether or not the goal is achieved. Because of the interconnectedness of all minds with the Higher Self, we need not fear that in pursuing our own real self-interest we will fail to contribute maximally to the real self-interest of others.

Since we look at all circumstances provided by the universe as unvalued feedback, life can now be felt as a deep, quiet knowing filled with joy and fulfillment. Oppression, criticism and failure are deleted from our new vocabulary, since these are merely examples of feedback moving us toward the path we most deeply desire for ourselves.

SEMCO

Semco is a Brazilian manufacturer of hydraulic pumps and generators that was on the verge of bankruptcy in 1980. Ricardo Semler became president of this company at that time and instituted a rather extreme, but karmically capitalistic, form of self-management characterized by distributed responsibility.

Three basic values dominate the company's paradigm. These are:

1.   Profit sharing. The workers receive 23 percent of after-tax profit.

2.   Information. Each employee has complete access to all vital information of the company, including the salaries of the top executives!

3.   Democracy. Workers can overrule any management decision by a majority vote.

Semco's 800 employees are treated like responsible adults.

They are put in the demanding position of using their own judgment and sense of responsibility. There are no time clocks; employees come and go according to their own schedules. There are no company dress codes, no company rules about travel expenses, no security searches or store-room padlocks. Managers are evaluated by their subordinates. Important decisions are made with company-wide participation.

The employees of Semco set their own working hours, and this includes the factory personnel. Most of their management people set their own salaries and bonuses, and all employees have complete access to the company books.

Three employees are elected in each division by their peers to invest the money in the profit sharing plan until the entire division meets and decides by majority vote exactly how these funds should be used for the production of additional income.

Semco found out from experience that the most productive number of employees in a unit consists of about 150 people. This is similar to the philosophy of the Gore corporation discussed earlier. This number of employees appears to be ideal in keeping each employee in touch with one another to assure maximum productivity and efficiency.

Ricardo says of this 150 maximum employee rule:

"For more than five million years, they [our ancestors] refined their ability to work in groups of no more than about a dozen people. Then along comes the industrial revolution, and suddenly workers are trying to function efficiently in factories that employ hundreds and even thousands. Organizing those hundreds into teams of about ten members each may help some, but there's still a limit to how many small teams can work well together."

Other unique and karmically capitalistic aspects of Semco include:

• Important policy decisions are made by a democratic vote throughout the entire company. An example of this principle dealt with the selection of a location for Semco's marine division. The management put forth a certain location that was rejected by the employees. It was decided through this democratic process to buy another building. The workers designed the layout for the equipment and hired one of Brazil's most well known artists to paint the entire facility, including the machinery.

• All manuals, rules, regulations and norms are abolished. Common sense is used throughout this organization. Semler states, "Common sense is a riskier tactic because it requires personal responsibility. It also requires just a touch of civil disobedience every time someone calls attention to something that's not working. We had to free the Thoreaus and the Tom Paines in the factory and come to terms with the fact that civil disobedience was not an early sign of revolution but a clear indication of common sense at work."

• It is not uncommon for employees to earn more than their supervisors.

• Promotions and hiring requires interviews and approval by all their future subordinates. Subordinates review their managers twice yearly.

Semco today is one of Brazil's fastest growing corporate karmic capitalists.

PATAGONIA

In northern California a manufacturer of high quality, rugged outdoor clothing named Patagonia places far more emphasis on solving environmental problems than on profit. It's founder, Yvon Chouinard states, "The more profit we make the more we can give away. Today the only profits we pull out of the company, 10 percent before taxes, go to environmental causes."

Chouinard believes that the company attracts employees "who wouldn't have come to work for us if we didn't give money away. Our CEO came from the Yosemite Institute and wouldn't have come to Patagonia if we hadn't had this philosophy."

Although Chouinard considered selling his company during the 1980s, he decided to stay in order to guide the company toward becoming a positive force in solving environmental problems. Patagonia donates considerable funds to approximately 250 environmentally friendly organizations. The goal of Patagonia is to recycle 70 percent of all the waste produced by the company as well as in the homes of employees, and is actively enlisting other companies to do the same.

THE BODY SHOP INTERNATIONAL

A British corporation that sells cosmetics and personal care products has used value-led principles of karmic capitalism, rather than market-driven paradigms to demonstrate their respect for people, animals and the environment, while making a handsome profit. This company is called The Body Shop International and was founded by Anita Reddick.

With over 320 outlets from Australia to the Article Circle, this 125 million dollar-a-year company does not advertise, fills its shelves with plain bottles containing soaps, scents, lotions and shampoos that don't promise beauty or youth but pledge only to "cleanse, polish, and protect the skin and hair," and does no animal testing. All employees are encouraged to become involved within the community on company time. This is a franchise company with a waiting list of over 5,000 in England alone. Potential franchises must show an environmental concern to be considered for a franchise.

We can quickly see that The Body Shop practices what it preaches in its involvement with the following organizations:

• It has funded a Boy's Town and training school for destitute children in Southern India.

• It supports a papermaking plant in Nepal where women make scented drawer liners from banana leaves and water hyacinths.

• It contributes to Greenpeace.

• Donations are made to Friends of the Earth.

• It spent one million dollars funding a hospital to develop artificial skin for burn victims.

In addition, this corporate karmic capitalist continually educates their employees on body care, drugs, urban cultures, AIDS issues and many others. Employees are encouraged to express their own creativity and initiative.

Posters in the stores urge the staff to "Break the Rules" and "Think Frivolously" and bonuses are paid for innovative suggestions.

SATURN

In chapter 1 I described a rather spiritually uplifting story of karmic capitalism that took place in a New Mexico Saturn dealership. General Motors invested five-billion dollars to create Saturn Corporation in the early 1980s. This was the world's largest "startup" company ever. It's paradigm consisted of creating a non-hierarchical company, which removed all "bosses" and placed operational decision making in the hands of the working teams. This had the effect of creating a work environment that encouraged shared cooperation.

MOTOROLA

Motorola has built into its culture the things that make the high-tech companies attractive places to work. Headquartered in Schaumburg, Illinois, this giant karmic corporate capitalist prides itself on its policy of open communication. There are over 95,000 employees in this company. All employees are on teams and each team has one of its members on a steering committee at the next higher level in the company. These committees permit and encourage information exchange upward, downward and laterally, and allow shop floor issues to reach highest management after going through only four levels in the chain.

An honor system was instituted in Motorola back in the 1950s, with all time clocks discarded. The employees of Motorola were among the first in a large U.S. corporation to gain a measure of job security: A decision by the CEO was—and still is—required to fire any worker with ten years or more service in the company. At that time this company was a relatively low-tech company with about a quarter of its business in consumer electronics, primarily car radios and Quasar televisions.

Robert Galvin was the CEO who in the late 1960s foresaw that Motorola's future was in higher-technology products, such as semiconductors and microprocessors. The problem was that their competitors, Texas Instruments, Intel and others, had a tremendous technological lead on Motorola.

By formulating a 10-year plan, anticipating the need for future change even though the company was not in any imminent trouble, the karmic capitalist Galvin realized he needed the complete cooperation of all of his employees. To compete with the Japanese required high standards of quality, productivity, cost and inventory control, customer service, and delivery.

A centralized highly directive corporate structure would not produce the kind of commitment, effort, and innovation needed to succeed. What was initiated was a decentralized organization with many new "presidents," each with a small entrepreneurial business to run as he saw fit. A generous bonus pool that rewarded innovation, risk taking, and superior performance was created, in addition to an incentive plan for managers.

This Participative Management Program (PMP) was begun in the 1970s, in which any idea proposed by a team member that leads to a cost reduction or to production that exceeds a target, all team members share in the gains through bonuses that can amount to 41 percent of base salary. The principle that the people in each pool are responsible for their own performance is measured by the production costs and materials use that are directly controllable by the team, was unheard of for a company the size of Motorola.

Motorola proved to be the company with the world's largest employee participation plan, and boasts significant productivity improvement, increased cooperation, decreased employee turnover and impressive cost reductions. It has resulted in better communication between all levels, which encourages people to work together toward common objectives. Needless to say, Motorola used its karmic capitalistic wisdom to attain and maintain its status of industry leader in semiconductors and microprocessors.

THE GRAMEEN BANK

In 1983 Muhammad Yunus opened up a bank in Bangladesh called the Grameen Bank. The term grameen means rural or village in Bengali, and the main purpose of this bank is to make loans to poor people who would otherwise not qualify for such funding.

Yunus refers to the small loans he makes to poor people to assist them in establishing their own businesses as micro loans. Initially, Yunus required borrowers to form groups of five, evaluate each other's loan proposals at weekly meetings and submit these loan requests to Grameen.

The policy of this bank was simply that if one group member defaults on payments, no other group member would be entitled to obtain additional loans until the debt was paid. Each group elected a president and treasurer through a democratic process. In addition, they were required to adhere to "16

Decisions" that were designed to improve both the lives of them and their families.

The "16 Decisions" can be summarized as follows:

1.   We shall follow and advance the four principles of Grameen Bank – discipline, unity, courage and hard work – in all walks of our lives.

2.   We shall bring prosperity to our families.

3.   We shall not live in dilapidated houses. We shall repair our houses and work toward constructing new houses as soon as possible.

4.   We shall grow vegetables all year round. We shall eat plenty of them and sell the surplus.

5.   During the plantation season, we shall plant as many seedlings as possible.

6.   We shall plan to keep our families small. We shall minimize our expenditures. We shall look after our health.

7.   We shall educate our children and ensure that we can earn to pay for their education.

8.   We shall always keep our children and their environment clean.

9.   We shall build and use pit-latrines.

10.   We shall drink water from tube wells. If it is not available, we shall boil water or use alum.

11.   We shall not take dowry at our son's weddings, nor shall we give any dowry at our daughter's weddings. We shall keep our center free from the curse of the dowry. We shall not practice child marriage.

12.   We shall not inflict any injustice on anyone, nor shall we allow anyone else to do so.

13.   We shall collectively undertake large investments for higher incomes.

14.   We shall always be ready to help each other. If anyone is in difficulty, we shall help him or her.

15.   If we come to know of any breach of discipline in any center, we shall go there and help restore discipline.

16.   We shall introduce physical exercises in all of our centers. We shall take part in all social activities collectively.

Grameen members in the U.S. and over 50 countries utilize this basis of functioning. Local chapters have modified this paradigm to suit their particular needs. The combination of encouraging entrepreneurial pursuits, along with these 16 Decisions qualifies Grameen Bank to join the ranks of corporate karmic capitalism.

The Grameen Bank became established in America when Yunus was approached by the Ford Foundation in 1985. The following year the Women's Self Employment Project (WSEP) was founded in Chicago. It set up a fund for low-income entrepreneurs.

WSEP's president Connie Evans created the Full Circle Fund in Chicago in 1988, using the Grameen Bank as a model. The maximum loan from the Full Circle Fund is $25,000, compared to $625.00 in Banna Houlla Village in Bangladesh, for example. By 1995 there were 60,000 participants in the U.S. in Grameen-style programs.

More than 10 million people worldwide have benefited from Yunus' concept. Yunus began this karmic capitalistic enterprise when he taught economics at a university in Bangladesh. He loaned twenty-seven dollars to poor individuals to begin their businesses. They all paid him back. He learned from these experiences that poor people were good credit risks.

Since the banking system is designed to keep poor people out, Yunus relied more on energy, good faith, vision and good principles to live by to qualify his applicants. Besides, his research revealed that more affluent people were more likely to default on loans. Poor people are better money managers, and know how to stretch what little money they have.

What began in 1971 as a small personal experiment matured into a Bangladesh approved and chartered bank and finally manifested as a worldwide revolution in banking.

LINCOLN ELECTRIC

Lincoln Electric Company has been manufacturing arc welding machines and electrodes since 1934. This Cleveland, Ohio corporate karmic capitalist rewards their employees for production, as well as creative and entrepreneurial behavior. Annual bonuses are paid for quality of work, output, cooperation and ideas to improve productivity.

Their bonus system doubles the annual income of the average worker. They even receive promotions if they devise a way to eliminate their own positions. At least thirty-two hours of work fifty weeks a year is guaranteed each employee.

Layoffs are unknown in this company. By "banking" new products during good times and releasing them on the market during a down phase of the business cycle, full employment is assured. Transferring employees from production into sales has also been used to prevent laying workers off.

Due to their effective cost reduction techniques (middle managers and supervisor positions no longer exist), productivity is double that of U.S. industrial workers in general, and the costs of their products has not greatly increased for several decades.

THE OLGA COMPANY

The manufacturer of women's undergarments located in Van Nuys, California pays their employees better than union wages and consistently out performs their competitors, who use sweatshop-like labor in Asia and Latin America.

Olga employees own shares of the company and participate in its profits. One of the more karmically capitalistic components of their profit-sharing plan is a "Profit Sharing Through Profit Caring" program. Profits are improved as a result of employee imagination, ingenuity and the participation of all line workers and managers.

Another interesting aspect of Olga's policy is the creation of jobs for underprivileged minority women. Approximately twenty-five percent of pretax profits are contributed to profit and stock-sharing plans.

HERMAN MILLER

One of America's largest manufacturers of office furniture is located in Zeeland, Michigan. With well over 3,500 employees, Herman Miller is a good size company. They removed all time clocks during the early 1950s.

In addition, employee participation is highly encouraged by a network of interlocking elected committees that discuss employee suggestions regarding corporate plans, problems, and opportunities. Bonuses are paid for suggestions or efforts of workers that reduce costs. Four different categories of goals are negotiated in committees. These goals are effective use of materials, labor, money and customer service. Bonuses are presented to employees who surpass their goals.

Other worker incentives include:
- A generous stock ownership plan.
- Complete sharing of managerial information.
- The company's "assumptions about work" motto.

This can be stated as follows:

HERMAN MILLER ASSUMPTIONS	TRADITIONAL ASSUMPTIONS
Focus is on self-control and the authority of competence	Control is through the authority hierarchy
Emphasis on what is right, a problem-oriented approach	Emphasis on who is right, a power-centered scheme
Performance is self-expression and self-fulfillment	Performance is an act of obedience
Subordinates share responsibility	Subordinates are assistants
Power is held in reserve as derived from	Power is exercised by those in authority
Motivation comes from the work itself	Motivation is supposed to spring from loyalty to the organization

- Employees participate in decision making and in corporate profits.
- A model system exists for communication between management and line workers and vice versa.

CONTROL DATA

Control Data has initiated a "ring of defense" program to insure stability for their employees. The nine rings of this program can be summarized as follows:

1. The regular introduction of new products.
2. Encouraging the retirement of employees to allow for more growth for younger workers.

3. A healthy use of part-time employees. Some of their working mothers have work hours from nine to three in order to care for school-age children, others who work from three to six after school, some who just work weekends, and still others who work two- and three-day weeks.

4. The use of independent contractors. These contractors are not terminated due to slow phases in the business cycle if this worker is dependent on Control Data for more than twenty-five percent of its business, a minority firm or employs the handicapped.

5. Hiring prisoners as subcontractors.

6. Moving employees from one division into another.

7. Offering the summer off to employees without pay.

8. Voluntary time off without pay.

9. Involuntary days off, for example, by closing the plants for a week during the Fourth of July and Thanksgiving without pay.

Control data builds all of their new factories in urban ghettos, assists poor small farmers and subsidizes undercapitalized small businesses of all types.

One of this corporate karmic capitalist's strong points is in the development of training programs for their employees that they then turned around and sold to other companies. They have also developed training programs for sale to others that they then turned around and made available to their own employees. Training is an integral component of each of the over 60,000 employee positions Control Data has filled all around the world.

The teaching machine used to train employees is called PLATO. Any subject that you can learn by drill can be taught on a PLATO computer terminal. PLATO has been used to retrain production workers to deal with such new technologies as computers and robots. American Airlines purchased a PLATO program to train its pilots. The self-teaching aspect of PLATO allows the employee to learn at their own pace, once a level of knowledge is established by pretesting.

Workstation is an alternative work site program that enables people to work at home or at a satellite location. Another Control Data innovation is the establishment of a program to assist employees with personal problems. The Employee Advisory Resource (EAR) is a twenty-four hour telephone hot line that is so successful that over 40,000 workers at more than 125 organizations in Minnesota have employed it. At anytime of the day or night employees experiencing disputes over company policies, problems with co-workers, marital difficulties or emotional mood swings can obtain help.

One of Control Data's finest examples of karmic capitalism took place in 1968 when they opened up a bindery in a depressed minority section of St.

Paul. They created a job-sharing system for 250 part-time employees, mostly young mothers and teenagers. The mothers work from 9 A.M. to 3 P.M. while their young children are in school, and the teenagers work the second shift, after school, from 3 P.M. to 6 P.M.

JOHNSON & JOHNSON

Johnson & Johnson's constitution is an example of a company's commitment to their shareholders. They list the people they are responsible to, followed by the specific obligation to each of them. These responsibilities are looked upon as mutually compatible and obtainable. Balance and symmetry are the rule.

The following is the Credo from Johnson & Johnson's constitution:

"We believe our first responsibility is to the doctors, nurses and patients, to mothers and all others who use our products and services. In meeting their needs everything we do must be of high quality. We must constantly strive to reduce our costs in order to maintain reasonable prices. Customers' orders must be serviced promptly and accurately. Our suppliers and distributors must have an opportunity to make a fair profit.

We are responsible to our employees, the men and women who work with us throughout the world. Everyone must be considered as an individual. We must respect their dignity and recognize their merit. They must have a sense of security in their jobs. Compensation must be fair and adequate, and working conditions clean, orderly and safe. Employees must feel free to make suggestions and complaints. There must be equal opportunity for employment, development and advancement for those qualified. We must provide competent management, and their actions must be just and ethical.

We are responsible to the communities in which we live and work to the world community as well. We must be good citizens—support good works and charities and bear out fair share of taxes. We must encourage civic improvements and better health and education. We must maintain in good order the property we are privileged to use, protecting the environment and natural resources.

Our final responsibility is to our stockholders. Business must make a sound profit. We must experiment with new ideas. Research must be carried on, innovative programs developed and mistakes paid for. New equipment must be purchased, new facilities provided and new products launched. Reserves must be created to provide for adverse times. When we operate according to these principles, the stockholders should realize a fair return."

We can see from this statement that the company has responsibilities to five different entities. These are: customers, employees, company, managers, local communities and shareholders. These central ideas represent a higher human purpose than simply improving the bottom line.

Johnson & Johnson will listen to their customers and initiate policies to better serve them. This karmic capitalist is a leader in basic research and includes ethical responsibilities for the welfare of its customers. A good example of the company's ethics occurred in September of 1982.

As a result of superior marketing, J & J positioned Tylenol to successfully compete with aspirin, Anacin and Bufferin throughout the 1970s. By 1978 Tylenol established itself as the best-selling drug in the U.S. In September of 1982 a psychotic laced Tylenol capsules with cyanide poison, and this resulted in the death of eight people.

The traditional (Old Guard) response would be to deny responsibility, stonewall, blame someone else and refuse interviews with the press. Even though J & J had no legal liability and did nothing wrong, they withdrew thirty-one million bottles of Tylenol, set up a toll-free hot line, made themselves accessible to the media and opened paths of communication with the health-care community.

By authentically apologizing and accepting responsibility for this tragedy, J & J emerged from the crisis as a champion of consumers. By early 1984, they had regained all of their market share.

Their management had done the right thing, and this resulted in a rapid regaining of public trust. Another example of their ethics took place when they researched the development of a "morning after" birth control pill. Many discussions concerning the morality of this product were held with theologians, philosophers and ethicists.

WHY THE OLD GUARD CORPORATIONS
WILL ULTIMATELY FAIL

We have seen that there are two basic activities in business: making and selling products or offering services. The most productive manner to accomplish this is to stimulate employees to take pride in their work. Lincoln Electric, Fel-Pro, Herman Miller, and Olga have become some of the most successful small-to-medium-sized companies in America.

The Old Guard states that these concepts of karmic capitalism cannot be applied to big business. But what about Motorola (with the world's biggest employee participation plan) or Control Data (with their employee entrepreneurship program) These companies illustrate the fact that big business can indeed apply successfully the principles of karmic capitalism.

By using sound financial controls, decentralization and commitment to technological innovation, a business of any size can become a corporate karmic capitalist. But the Old Guard won't consider this paradigm, so they are destined to mimic the fate of the dinosaurs. Here is why:

• The insensitivities to the environment in which they function will continually result in large financial losses. We can look back to RCA's marketing program with their Selectavision videodisc recorders against the vastly superior videocasette recorders and laser disc recorders as an example. Another example was General Motor's persistence in selling big cars in the middle of an oil crisis during the 1970s.

• The Old Guard miscalculates future trends. Exxon during the 1970s predicted that the price of oil would continue to escalate between 1980 and the year 2000 at the same rate it had increased following the Arab oil embargo of 1973. A twenty billion dollar investment in synthetic fuels was decided upon. These fuels would only be economical if the price of oil reacted as Exxon predicted.

By 1978 other futurists presented a different paradigm to Exxon's management. They proposed that oil prices would fall due to any one of four reasons: (1) conservation could reduce demand; (2) new oil discoveries could increase supply; (3) OPEC members could engage in under-the-table discounting, thus weakening the power of the cartel; or (4) in the long run, alternative energy sources (solar, wind, nuclear) might lessen the dependence on fossil fuels. We all know what happened to fuel prices during the 1980s. By 1982 Exxon lost one billion dollars on synthetic fuels and abandoned the program.

• The arrogance of the Old Guard. IBM in 1975 scoffed at the concept of a microprocessor——and computer miniaturization in general. At that time IBM had nearly three quarters of the nation's computer business, most of which involved mainframes and other large computers.

It took Apple's and other Silicon Valley companies' introduction of personal computers in the late 1970s to finally get IBM to take part in this market. They nearly missed the boat entirely due to their arrogance.

• The tendency for the Old Guard to engage in quick decisions and become impatient with the hard, time-consuming work of coping with ambiguous issues. Anything but action-oriented behavior is considered wishy-washy and discouraged.

•	The Old Guard think in the short term, repeat their past behavior and ignore the principle of change.

•	It is impossible to convince the Old Guard that the purpose of a corporation involves more than improving shareholder equity.

•	Single-mindedness is typical of the Old Guard. Although this tendency can provide for consistency of purpose and clarity of vision, it is outmoded in an age of rapid technological change and fickled consumers.

•	Relying too much on current customers is another failing of the Old Guard. No customer in the 1950s ever pushed RCA for color television. Du Pont was not solicited by its customers to invent nylon. Research and development by creative and right-brained scientists is what is needed to become an industry leader.

Corporate karmic capitalists will eventually replace the Old Guard in every type of business. When Lee Iacocca stated proudly, "We have one and only one ambition: to be the best. What else is there?", he was speaking as a karmic capitalist. One trend in American business is that few corporations have tried to be the very best in their field. This Old Guard mentality reflects the saying, "most of life is just showing up."

Few Old Guard companies allow junior management to challenge the higher levels of corporate policy makers. The Old Guard neither break new ground nor do they attempt to raise business practices to a higher plane. They do not try to be the best. Instead, they enjoy the less demanding role of "good old boys," who accept rather than challenge the comfortable paradigms and standards of the day.

In companies like Motorola you will frequently see managers challenging their superiors to rethink basic premises and unlearn outmoded techniques. Since our environment is constantly changing, corporate karmic capitalists are always striving to create a balance involving the shareholder's interests in the short term with investing in the future for the long term.

"THE TIMES THEY ARE A CHANGING"

According to Ralph H. Kilmann and Teresa Covin, "Corporate transformation is a process by which organizations examine what they were, what they are, what they will need to be, and how to make the necessary changes. Implementing those changes affects both psychological and strategic aspects of an organization. The term corporate is used to convey the comprehensive efforts required, in contrast to a piecemeal or single-division effort. Transformation indicates the fundamental nature of the change, in contrast to a mere linear extrapolation from the past. Corporate transformation is serious, large-scale change that demands new ways of perceiving, thinking, and behaving by all members of the organization."

In their book Corporate Transformation, editors Ralph Kilmann and Teresa Covin further state: "Corporate transformation is a new phenomenon. Never before in the history of the world have so many organizations had to question their very purpose, strategy, structure, and culture as they have had to do in the 1980s. No senior executives of any organization today could or would dispute that one of their major responsibilities is to revitalize their organizations for a competitive world."

Corporate karmic capitalism deals with business affecting global values. Business represents an important way to improve both ourselves and the world in which we live. We karmic capitalists enter the world of business not merely to become rich, but to become who we are. We are always attempting to improve spiritually our world in the process of exercising abundance principles.

In Vanguard Movement, James O'Toole selected those large U.S. Corporations that were both profitable and socially responsible. He called these "vanguard" in the belief that they could serve as future models for all large, publicly held corporations. Examples of vanguard corporations are Motorola, Control Data, Dayton-Hudson, John Deere, Honeywell, Levi Strauss, Atlantic-Richfield, and Weyerhaeuser.

These corporate karmic capitalist all strive for excellence in every aspect of their business. The belief that corporations effect the degrees of freedom and equality we all experience and that they greatly influence our standard of living and the quality of our lives is an important component in these vanguard companies. It is equally important to continually experiment with and implement new ways to manage organizations which will enhance social justice. Managers who stand fast with their high ideals, even in difficult times, resisting the temptation for short-term actions, being willing to risk taking an unpopular position in order to stand behind their purpose, and exhibiting moral courage at all costs are evident in these corporate karmic capitalists.

THE GOALS OF THE CORPORATE KARMIC CAPITALISTS

From the examples I presented, we can see certain common goals exhibited by corporate karmic capitalists. These may be listed as follows:

- The creation of a work environment in which people came together to do work that was fulfilling, and that promoted their own personal and professional development.
- Assisting individual employees to remove blocks to their intuition and creativity.
- Establishing an aura of shared responsibility.
- Striving to be the best in their industries.
- Valuing people at all times, with the assumption that profit will follow automatically.
- Creating fair and democratic compensation practices.
- Focus at all times on a strong sense of purpose.
- Fostering a feeling in each employee that they are contributing in some way to individual lives and to society.
- Shifting from a competitive, hierarchically dependent behavior to an interdependent, cooperative attitude; from considering work as a mean, by which some earn their living and others accumulate wealth, to envisioning work as an instrument for spiritual growth and global contributions to humanity.
- Creating an environment of open communication so that people feel free to speak up and feel confident that they will be told about critical information that affects their jobs and lives.

CHAPTER 10

KARMIC CAPITALISM IN THE 21ST CENTURY

The transformation I described in chapter 7 encompasses all of society. Business is already playing a major role in acting as a bridge between the old paradigms and the new thought. It has the effect of producing a smoother transition.

We can look at this paradoxical situation more closely. I have previously pointed out that there is no organization more flexible and adaptive than business. On the one hand, business represents the old paradigm of logic, rational thinking and obsession with material gain by encouraging over consumption of goods and services.

Yet, at the same time, the corporate sector has and is already responding to the existential crisis over the purpose and meaning of work and business. Those companies that adhere to the old paradigms of greed, arrogance and apathy will not survive. The organizations following karmic capitalistic principles of this new thought will not only survive, they will thrive.

Whereas the old way of thinking in business measured growth in strictly economic terms by an ever increasing rate of consumption, it ignored the big picture and attempted to resolve problems by focusing its attention on symptom only. This planning the future from the past and "bigger is better" mentality simply cannot survive in the twenty-first century.

Previous paradigms had no interest in intuition, merely evaluated and judged, exhibited a lack of tolerance, ignored emotions and left few opportunities for change and creative growth. This purpose of enterprise being solely the making of a profit, and the judgment of success based on how much money they made and/or possessions they owned, will go the same way as the dinosaurs—extinction.

The old thought placed great importance on power. This obsession only reflected their insecurities and fear of not succeeding. Since their value system was based solely on obsessions, even when they did "succeed" by their standards, they demonstrated fear of losing what they had acquired. Spirituality was either ignored, or mocked in the process. Hierarchical systems were built to insulate the upper level executives from this fear. This ensured control and functioned to prevent any threatening changes (including growth) from occurring.

Greed was also exhibited by these old paradigm businesspeople in making decisions to ensure a quick return on investments, rather than on the long-term needs of the company. Quarterly reports and dividends are examples of this short-sighted approach of living from one three month period to another.

Distancing ourselves from nature further characterized the old way of doing business. Even when these companies assisted the Third World developing their natural resources (oil, rain forests, etc.), it was done in a conditional form. A requirement was placed on this assistance, in that the receiving country had to purchase a certain amount of goods and services from them, or just simply allowed this raping of the Earth. These Third World countries watched as greedy Western businesses ruthlessly exploited their human and natural resources, instead of fostering growth of their culture.

The new thought exhibited by corporate karmic capitalism will encompass the entire planet with all of its inhabitants on an integrated and holistic scale. Both compassion and spirituality are now the norm in this vision. A raising of both human and the planet's consciousness will now be initiated.

Humans will no longer be separated from mother nature. When the expression "we" is used, it will include both our species, other life forms and the planet itself. This new paradigm will be tolerant, compassionate, devoid of value judgments and exhibit a balance between the male rational thinking approach and the female nurturing and feeling tendencies in business.

A trust in our feelings and intuition will also be characteristic of this new way of conducting business. At times a simple "knowing" of what is right and what doesn't work will be felt, without depending on surveys or research reports.

The heart of this paradigm will reflect the concept that the purpose of business, as well as life itself, is spiritual growth. Everything else is secondary to this principle. We will recognize the fact that each of us are creators of our destinies. There is no such thing as good or bad luck, what we send out to the universe comes back to us. We are thus responsible for our actions and the subsequent results obtained.

Corporations in the twenty-first century will begin to do what is best for society as a whole. The aspects of life that promote joy and meaning to our earthly sojourn will be emphasized. A setting free of our inner resources of creativity and spirituality will take hold in global society. The expansion of human potential by linking the wisdom from our Higher Self will be a critical component of this mechanism.

The new thought will consist simply of the principle that the main function and purpose for business is to encourage the personal and spiritual development of its employees, while at the same time bettering the universe in which we all live. Profits will be made, but not at the expense of human development. A process, rather than result, orientation will be the rule.

All aspects of these businesses of the future, including research and development, manufacturing, interactions with "competitors" and the public, will be directed toward this encouragement of a global consciousness of spiritual growth.

Twenty-first century businesses will function within a paradigm that every human being is both unique and a part of all other humans. Fear of failure, competition per se, power struggles and overly complex hierarchies will cease to exist.

Hierarchies represent power struggles. These systems are constructed on a lack of trust and fear foundation. The climate of petty politics and competition created inhibits creativity and results in wasted energy and resources. Both inflexibility and inertia are built into this system, and it simply won't survive.

The crumbling of these hierarchies will begin from those near the bottom. As new, young talent select only those companies representing karmic capitalistic paradigms (as we have seen, these companies already exist), the old thought organizations will have to implement radical changes, or simply perish.

This is not to imply that companies of the future will not contain managers or leaders. These executives will not be appointed on the basis of power or seniority, but by merit. Now everyone in the organization will be equally responsible for its success.

Leaders in businesses of the future will be selected by mutual agreement among the employees. The track record of these individuals will be a key factor, but there will be no election to office. They will simply be called upon to assume certain leadership responsibilities. It is solely up to this potential leader or manager to accept or reject this opportunity.

The leader of the future has no external power per se, nor are they at the top of some artificial hierarchy. This individual functions from within the midst of the corporation and coordinates its overall operation. It is only when specifically asked to decide on a certain issue do they present their opinions.

These coordinators replace the former "bosses" of the past. Since the corporation functions to stimulate the spiritual growth and development of its employees, the responsibilities of these coordinators are far broader than these of leaders of the past.

Dispensing information will be an important component of the coordinator's responsibilities. In addition to keeping all employees up to date on their own individual activities and responsibilities, an openness toward information concerning the entire company will be disseminated. This is part of the new integration and holistic approach to commerce.

Job rotation will be a part of this paradigm, in that no position will be thought of as more attractive than another. By allowing others to also function as coordinators, everyone benefits from this shared responsibility, and petty jealousies are eliminated. Each employee now gains a thorough understanding of the company and the meaning and purpose of its goals.

The old business paradigm incorporates many middlemen between functionaries, which results in distancing employees from each other and most importantly from the consumer. Another disadvantage of this system is that it hinders creativity.

We may consider each management division within a company as a middleman. There are a plethora of rules as to how to handle questions and problems within this hierarchy. Many creative ideas are lost through this maze of insulation before they could be heard by top management.

We find middlemen functioning as personnel supervisors, who act as arbitrators with employee problems, instead of allowing a proper resolution by those directly involved. Unions are an even better example of this middleman mentality.

Corporate karmic capitalists of the future will be characterized by an absence of hierarchies and a significant decrease, if not complete abolishment, of middlemen. Since sales and marketing departments contain traditionally the highest percentage of middlemen, here is where the greatest reduction in these functionaries will be noted.

The customers will want direct contact with the manufacturers in the future. This paradigm is already in existence as exemplified by trade fairs, local grocery markets (Farmer's markets) and the car manufacturer Volvo. Volvo now is experimenting with manufacturing a car from beginning to end without the traditional assembly line production teams.

Car buyers of the future will be able to be in direct contact with the manufacturer before, during and after its assembly. This situation would only instill higher quality cars.

An openness to all of the company's information by each employee will be the rule in the future. There will be no secrets or hidden agendas. As information now will go directly from the source to the employee requesting it, a more direct form of contact is established between the workers. This openness applies to both internal dealings and global company functioning.

The businesses of the twenty-first century will also be far more flexible than ever before. This will come about as a result of the elimination of hierarchies. Now there will no longer be a natural resistance to change. A new striving for personal development will replace the former obsession with making as much money as possible in the shortest amount of time, with the least amount of concern to its employees or society as a whole.

These futuristic enterprises will not be characterized by goals or plans per se. Instead, a shared vision will dominate the company's direction. We must understand the fact we set goals, but we have visions.

Visions originate from feelings, and represents a longing for life characterized by both inner and outer harmony. When we discuss visions we are describing an inner desire originating from our Higher Self for something we want to see manifested in reality.

A vision is abstract and without form. Although it does point us in a certain direction, it is not measurable in terms of quantity and time. We most certainly can say that a vision has a life of its own, and is perpetually growing and moving throughout the course of its duration.

These concepts we call visions realize themselves. Our subconscious translates information from our Higher Self in the form of vision to focus our attention in a certain direction.

Whereas goals are derived from logical think processes, visions emerge from feelings. Goals may come about from analytical and mechanical functions. They are time-bound and concrete, static and have no life of their own. Visions, on the other hand, are continuously moving and lead to growth and development by having a life of its own.

Corporate karmic capitalists of the future will operate by means of visions, not goals. These visions will be communicated to all employees of the company, so that it contains the appropriate strength and support to be realized.

We can only live a vision. It cannot be checked on or fed into a computer.

Since a vision is an ongoing process of growth, the more conscientious we are at living our visions, the faster they become realized.

The central focal point of these businesses of the future will be people, not production of goods and services. This organization exists to serve its employee contributors and not the other way around. It functions not to exploit markets, but to serve them.

We may consider the starting point for these companies as the consumer's need for goods and services. Consumers instruct the company how and with which products they can best be served. There is a cooperative working communication and relationship between consumers and the businesses that manufacture these products.

The work produced by these employees now begins to take on new meaning, as it effectively serves humankind. Since both the company and the work it authorized has an inward and outward meaning, a new UP-3 paradigm emerges globally.

Service functions of these futuristic enterprises take on new dimensions. Traditional companies used services as a marketing tool following purchase of a product as a form of after-market income. With new thought companies, these services will be an expression of the company's care and concern for the customer and the goods produced.

By assuring the products manufactured will be used in the best possible manner, the customer now will obtain the particular goods that best suit their needs. This new paradigm view life itself as a developmental process in which we grow spiritually as the universe presents us with opportunities. The process of life itself is the meaning, not the money, fame, power or possessions acquired during this sojourn.

Commerce is just another method of learning and obtaining these necessary experiences. It is only one of several methods of our growth as a soul. Recreational activities, time with our family, helping others and so on provide other avenues for us to learn and better our lives and those of the rest of the planet.

Empowerment is fostered, as we determine what is best for ourselves, instead of depending on some corporate authority. Work now has no greater importance in our lives than any other aspect of our being.

This will bring the end of obsessive-compulsive workaholics and power-driven self-centered businesspeople showing nothing but a selfish and arrogant "me first" attitude toward others.

Everything is interrelated with every other component of life. We are a part of every other human being, so that each new growth benefits everyone else, in addition to ourselves. The total knowledge of the world expands with each new insight. The more each citizen invests in themselves, the greater their contribution to the global society.

With this emphasis on openness, flexibility, closeness and compassion, the new companies create a nidus of the elimination of hierarchies, waste, petty politics and greed. A deeper meaning of life is one consequence of this new paradigm. Our focus is altered from an outer to an inner growth. Our Higher Selves play a pivotal role in this futuristic orientation to business.

The 21st century will see a major change in the workplace. Democracy now becomes an integral component of the organization's functioning. A great deal of respect for the abilities and dignity of the worker will now be evident.

Assumptions made by corporate leaders will include:
- Employees are truly motivated to do their best.
- Workers have earned the right to be viewed as responsible and intelligent people capable of contributing to the decision process.
- Each individual employee is competent at their job.
- The employee needs to have access to information about the company to make better decisions.
- Each worker has unique goals, needs and the company must provide avenues to stimulate the employees skill, creativity and thought processes.

Corporate karmic capitalists of the future allows employees to design their own career paths and work environment as far as this is practical. Workers are no longer controlled or commanded, and a continual reference is made to the big picture and core ideas that govern this company.

These karmic capitalists in turn provide the following for their investors:
- A steady and competitive return on investment. This return on their investment is consistent with the risk and with competitive opportunities.
- Treating investors as if they were the actual long-term owners of the firm.
- Providing long-term growth of equity.
- Managing operations as prudently, efficiently, and productively as possible. This includes the conducting of business in a manner that fosters long-term preferred-customer/preferred-supplier relationships.
- Management of the Company in a financially prudent manner, pursuing stability and continuity of operation, in order to be a good corporate citizen.

In addition, the following practices concerning change will be commonplace in the corporate world:

•   Philosophies will not be set, but will evolve over time and grow out of experience.

•   Changes will be made within the very heart of the organization. This change will be a continual process.

•   Long-term planning will initiate these changes. Each employee will be informed about the process, which will be divided into smaller tasks.

•   The upper levels of management will support these changes and make these commitments known throughout the company.

•   The shareholders and customers will be the primary source of these changes.

•   These changes will exhibit a consistency between objectives, strategies, rewards, structure, training, management style and control systems, since they are interrelated.

CONCLUSION

We can truly transform our lives on the physical plane into a spiritual voyage leading to the unfoldment of our soul. This form of psychic empowerment and repowerment is part of our karmic purpose.

It is well within the universe's plan for each one of us to benefit through abundance, while this spiritual unfoldment occurs. Our incentive is only heightened to continue with this process as we continually receive rewards. This is the heart of karmic capitalism.

Our free will is the determining factor that allows this paradigm to be one of bliss or a struggle. By selecting the path of spiritual growth, you begin a mission to align your soul both with your true karmic purpose and the universe's big picture.

In addition to a more meaningful and productive life, other benefits will be experienced by you as you follow this system to its natural conclusion. These additional benefits include:

- Increased creativity.
- Good fortune in all aspects of your life.
- Better relationships with greater honesty and openness.
- Reduced stress.
- Improved health and resistance to disease, both physical and mental.
- The attainment of abundance.
- Spiritual growth, accompanied by feelings of peace, inner joy and love.

As you allow this process of spiritual unfoldment to take place, life becomes more meaningful. The full beauty of the universe and all of its wonders are revealed as you learn to release your fears and embrace unconditional love. The rate of your enlightenment depends upon your level of commitment and willingness to face your fears. Only your "heart-of-heart" effects can accomplish this goal of karmic capitalism.

As the ancients emphasized "know thy self." The superconscious mind tap stressed throughout this book will facilitate your accessing your Higher

Self and tapping into both the intuition and wisdom that originates from the fourth dimension of human consciousness.

Making contact with this fourth dimension and living the ethical life of a karmic capitalist removes the abundance barriers you may have experienced in the past. Both your business life and your world take on new meaning. A new empowered future awaits you.

Your beliefs play a major role in karmic capitalism. Do not look to the physical world alone for the keys to unlock the door to abundance. We create our reality entirely from our beliefs. If you desire to change your world and attract abundance, change your beliefs. I have presented several easy-to-use exercises to unleash the creative power of your subconscious to do just this.

Any suffering, frustration and emotional pain you may be currently experiencing are caused by fear-laden beliefs. Your fears are memories of past pain projected into the future. By bringing your subconscious negative beliefs into your conscious awareness and releasing them through cleansing, you empower and repower yourself to create a future without pain and one characterized by abundance.

Fear can only result in a withdrawal from life. Abundance requires an active expansion and renewal of both your desires and your soul's energy. Fears arise because of the imbalance between the energy of love in your soul and the energy of fear in your personality. This is an ideal time to take charge of your life, custom design your own destiny and enter the prosperity realm of karmic capitalism.

Most of us are conditioned to the cause and effect paradigm of science. This creates beliefs that the three-dimensional world we see daily is the only reality there is. Fortunately, this is not true, and by accessing the fourth dimension by way of our Higher Self we can fully understand the limitation of conventional science.

Since science fails to address our inner world of beliefs, thoughts and emotions in their cause and effect paradigms, all metaphysical and spiritual principles are ignored. The role of consciousness in creating our reality daily is only dealt with by quantum physics, and most conventional scientists scoff at that discipline. Scientists mostly brush aside all theories involving the holistic integration of body, mind and soul.

Spirituality is derived from the word spirit, which The American Heritage Dictionary defines as "the vital principle or animating force traditionally believed to be within living beings." How can we become psychically empowered (or repowered) unless we possess this vital principle or animating force within our being? The answer is simple, we can't.

What we should consider is not whether we are spiritual beings, but exactly just what are our beliefs as spiritual beings. The beliefs you hold about the nature of business and of life will determine how you will manage your career. Allowing beliefs that you cannot attain abundance, or the world is evil and the classic reward and punishment paradigm is the only system, severely limits your growth as a soul.

Karmic capitalism cannot be attained with outmoded and limiting beliefs. You must now believe in a loving universe that offers plenty of opportunities to attract and attain abundance, and this universe truly wants you to succeed.

Incorporating the principles and practices put forth in this book will place you on the road to abundance and spiritual growth. This is karmic capitalism. By tapping into your inner wisdom (Higher Self) you are freeing yourself from the confines of the three-dimensional world, and this will foster your ability to find creative solutions to business problems, take better risks and make more competent decisions.

Karmic capitalists will be the forerunner of the business world of the twenty-first century. They unquestionably function on an ethical and moral basis and the companies they create will be derived form a genuine desire and commitment to serve the universe.

Spirituality entails the sacrificing of one's selfish personal needs and desires to assist in the universe's game plan. The question you need to ask yourself is do you have the karmic muscle to be a part of this system? Are you willing to do the hard work, prescribed throughout this book, of becoming aware of your Higher Self, of releasing those that no longer serve you, and of finding new and deeper ways of relating to your workplace, your life, and the universe through the process of permanently altering your belief system?

As a karmic capitalist your life will be one characterized more by questions than answers. You will often be exposed to criticism and less evolved souls. The universe will constantly test you, and you will often stand alone. The good news is that your world will be opened up to an unlimited range of possibilities, in which abundance and spiritual growth dominate.

By accessing our Higher Self, we make choices representing our inner being and perfect energy component. We are true to ourselves and an asset to the universe. This allows us to fulfill that part of us that longs for completion within the universe's design. That is true spirituality. You must give yourself permission to develop your spirituality and bring it into the marketplace. When this is accomplished all will benefit in a win-win-win manner.

Always bear in mind that the universe has plans for you that far exceed anything you might have considered. Using the principles of karmic capitalism will bring to fruition people in your professional and personal life who respect you and circumstances that will support your abundance goals. You are truly a force to be reckoned with.

You are reading this to attain abundance. Your definitions of no doubt success encompass a certain materialist component. Karmic capitalism is a most efficient answer to your quest. Always keep in mind that success is a journey and not merely a destination. The process is as important as the result.

We have seen corporate karmic capitalism manifested in the workplace as companies possessing many of the following characteristics:

- Companies owned solely by the employees.
- A business life that is no longer production oriented, but, instead, focuses on giving back to the community and global society.
- Work with personal and human development as its primary purpose.
- Companies without any hierarchy or concentrations of power.
- Businesses with the primary purpose of serving human development.
- Companies serving the market instead of exploiting it.
- Work environments that stimulate creativity and assist employees in removing blocks to intuition and creativity.
- Companies that do not strive to amass wealth and build economic value, but instead use their excess means to give energy to the process of their employees' personal development.
- Companies providing an environment of shared responsibility.
- Work environments practicing open communication and that focus on a strong sense of purpose continually striving to be the very best in their industry.
- Companies instituting fair and democratic compensation practices.
- Companies combining spiritual growth with abundance principles.

Research on human consciousness has demonstrated the perceptual bias of Western industrial society in relationship to exploring spirituality in the workplace. It is our own resistance to these paradigms that have resulted to limiting beliefs that certain things shouldn't happen.

When it comes to applying the ancients concept of "know thyself," the best laid plans of using affirmations and visual imagery to reprogram our subconscious often goes astray. The defense mechanisms are very skillful at causing us to "forget" to practice the exercises (as presented in this book) to attain karmic capitalism.

Since Western culture has thoroughly trained us not to trust ourselves, it is up to you to take special efforts to play your self-hypnosis tapes and practice the other exercises presented in this book. It is about time to trust yourself in that your Higher Self knows what you most deeply desire (karmic purpose) and precisely how to attain this goal by resolving all current conflicts and obstacles in your path toward karmic capitalism.

It is now time to trust yourself so that you may know yourself and discover your talents and highest potential of creativeness. We need not cling to old limiting beliefs that certain things shouldn't happen. There are two ways to be fooled: one is to believe what isn't so; the other is to refuse to believe what is so.

If we truly want to have more control over our futures and attain abundance, we must change the way we think about ourselves and the universe. Altering our beliefs through subconscious reprogramming and superconscious mind taps represents the first step toward leading a fuller and more satisfying life. This book was attempted to detail specific ways to accomplish these goals and allow you to enter the realm of karmic capitalism.

Always bear in mind that specific goals are required to use this system effectively. You absolutely must have a clear-cut vision of what you desire and where you want to be to attain financial independence.

Vague goals such as "I want a better job" or "I would like to make a lot of money" simply won't work. Detail the position you desire in job description, location, salary range, and so on. If you desire a certain net worth or annual income, spell it out precisely. Your Higher Self and subconscious will do the rest.

Utilizing the exercises presented herein to develop your spirituality allows you to create a win-win-win situation, and this is the basis of karmic capitalism. Approach all tasks with total optimism and an absolute belief that you will succeed and the universe will be better off as a result of your efforts.

Keep a positive view of human nature, and maintain the attitude that no matter how much the odds may be against success, you can accomplish anything you set your subconscious/
superconscious mind to.

Act in a decisive and efficient, yet compassionate, manner in all aspects of your life. Keep busy and never forget that the acquisition of knowledge is a never-ending process. Never rest on your intellectual laurels. Learning is always a process, not an event.

I hope that the principles and exercises presented in this book assist you in developing your spirituality and abundance mentality. Be conscientious about your efforts in attaining the status of karmic capitalist. My interest is always to support you in facilitating the creation of an ideal reality for you. Feel free to contact my office with questions, comments, or just to share your own story. I am open to your point of view, and truly desire this relationship to be a win-win-win one. My reason is simple: I am a karmic capitalist.

BIBLIOGRAPHY

Adams, John, ed. Transforming Work. Alexandria, VA: Miles River Press, 1984.

Bateson, Gregory. Steps to an Ecology of Mind. New York: Ballantine, 1972.

Birch, D. Job Creation in America. New York: Free Press, 1987.

Bohn, D. Unfolding Meaning. London: Ark Paperbacks, 1987.

Branden, N. The Six Pillars of Self Esteem. New York: Bantam Books, 1994.

Canfield, J. Hansen, M. V., et al. Chicken Soup for the Soul at Work. Deerfield Beach, Florida: Health Communications, Inc. 1996.

Capra, Fritjof. The Turning Point: Science, Society, and the Rising Culture. New York: Bantam Books, 1982.

Chouinard, Y. "Coming of Age—Yvon Chouinard." Inc. Magazine, April, 1988.

Counts, Alex. Give Us Credit. New York: Times Books, 1996.

Daly, Herman, and Cobb, J.B. For the Common Good: Rededicating the Economy Toward Community, the Environment, and a Sustainable Future. Boston: Beacon Press, 1989.

Durning, A. T. How Much Is Enough?: The Consumer Society and the Future of the Earth. New York: W. W. Norton and Company, 1992.

Emery, Stewart. The Owner's Manual for Your Life. Doubleday & Co., 1982.

Eysenck, H. J. Explaining the Unexplained: Mysteries of the Paranormal. Garden City, N.Y.: Avery, 1993.

Ferguson, Marilyn. The Aquarian Conspiracy: Personal and Social Transformation in the 1980s. Los Angeles: Jeremy Tarcher, 1980.

Fields, Rick. Chop Wood Carry Water: A Guide to Finding Spiritual Fulfillment in Everyday Life. Los Angeles: Jeremy Tarcher, 1984.

Gershon, D. and Straub, G. Empowerment: The art of creating your life as you want it. New York: Dell Publishing, 1989.

Giles, Lionel. The Analects of Confucius. Bloomington, IN: The Eastern Press, 1976.

Goldberg, Bruce. Past Lives-Future Lives. New York: Ballantine Books, 1988.

_____. Soul Healing. St. Paul: Llewellyn Pub., 1996.

_____. Peaceful Transition: The Art of Conscious Dying and the Liberation of the Soul. St. Paul: Llewellyn Pub., 1997.

_____. Self-Hypnosis: Easy Ways to Hypnotize Your Problems Away. Franklin Lakes, NJ: New Page Books, 2001.

_____. New Age Hypnosis. St. Paul: Llewellyn, 1998.

_____. Protected by the Light: The Complete Book of Psychic Self-Defense. Tucson, AZ: Hats Off Books, 1999.

_____. Ascension: The Art of Soul Perfection and the Attainment of Grace. Sun Lakes, AZ: Book World, Inc. 2004.

_____. Dream Your Problems Away: Heal Yourself While You Sleep. Franklin Lakes, NJ: New Page Books, 2003.

_____. Past Lives, Future Lives Revealed. Franklin Lakes, NJ: New Page Books, 2004.

Harrison, R. "Strategies for a New Age." Human Resource Management, 1983 22 (3), 209-235.

Hawken, P. Growing a Business. New York: Fireside, 1987.

Hawking, S. A Brief History of Time. New York: Bantam Books, 1988.

Kilmann, R. H.; Covin, Teresa, et. al. Corporate Transformation. San Francisco: Jossey-Bass, 1988.

Lashley, K. In Search of the Engram in Physiological Mechanisms in Animal Behavior. New York: Academic Press, 1950.

Levering, R. "Paradise, Corporate-Style." Business Month, 1988, Jul/Aug., 47-50.

Maccoby, Michael, Why Work: Leading the New Generation. New York: Simon and Schuster, 1988.

Mollner, Terry. Mondragon: The Journey From the Material Age to the Relationship Age Has Begun. New York: Doubleday & Co., 1990.

Muller, Robert. New Genesis: Shaping a Global Spirituality. New York: Doubleday & Co., 1982.

Mumford, L. The transformations of Man. New York: Harper and Brothers, 1956.

Naisbitt, J. and Aburdene, P. Re-inventing the Corporation. New York: Warner, 1985.

Needleman, Jacob. Money and the Meaning of Life. New York: Doubleday & Co., 1991.

Ornstein, Robert, and Ehrlich, Paul. New World, New Mind. New York: Doubleday & Co., 1989.

O'Toole, J. Vanguard Management: Redesigning the Corporate Future. New York: Doubleday & Co., 1985.

Pascarella, P. The New Achievers. New York: Free Press, 1984.

Phillips, Michael. The Seven Laws of Money. Menlo Park, Calif.: Word Wheel, 1974.

Ray, Michael, and Rochelle Myers. Creativity in Business. New York: Doubleday & Co., 1986.

Robertson, James. Future Wealth: A New Economics for the 21st Century. London: Cassell Publishers, Inc., 1990.

Rossner, John. In Search of the Primordial Tradition. St. Paul: Llewellyn Publications, 1989.

Saltzman, Amy. Downshifting: Reinventing Success on a Slower Track. New York: Harper Collins, 1991.

Semler, R. "Managing without managers." Harvard Business Review, 19869, 67 (5), 76-84.

Senge, Peter. The Fifth Discipline. New York: Doubleday & Co, 1990.

Shames, Laurence. The Hunger for More: Searching for Values in an Age of Greed. New York: Times Books, 1989.

Sinetar, M. "The Actualized Worker." Futurist, Mar./Apr., 1987, 21-25.

Smith, H. W. The 10 Natural Laws of Successful Time and Life Management: Proven strategies for increased productivity and inner peace. New York: Warner Books, 1994.

Toffler, A. The Third Wave. New York: Bantam, 1981.

Toynbee, Arnold. A Study of History. London: Oxford University Press, 1935.

Veblen, Thorstein. The Theory of the Leisure Class. New York: Penguin Books, 1994.

Wall Street Journal. "Personal Bankruptcies." June 18, 1991.

Wilber, Ken. Eye to Eye. New York: Anchor Books, 1983.

Wilhelm, Richard (translator) and Cary F. Baynes. The I Ching. Princeton, N.J.: Princeton University Press, 1950.

Woodward, Harry and Buchholz, Steve. Aftershock: Helping People Through Corporate Change. New York: John Wiley & Sons, 1987.

ABOUT THE AUTHOR

Dr. Bruce Goldberg holds a B.A. degree in Biology and Chemistry, is a Doctor of Dental Surgery, and has an M.S. degree in Counseling Psychology. He retired from dentistry in 1989, and has concentrated on his hypnotherapy practice in Los Angeles. Dr. Goldberg was trained by the American Society of Clinical Hypnosis in the techniques and clinical applications of hypnosis in 1975.

Dr. Goldberg has interviewed on *Coast to Coast AM*, *Oprah*, *Leeza, Joan Rivers, Regis*, *Tom Snyder, Jerry Springer, Jenny Jones*, and *Montel Williams* shows; by *CNN, NBC, Fox, CBS News*, and many others.

Through lectures, television and radio appearances, and newspaper articles, *including interviews in Time* The *Los Angeles Times*, *USA Today*, and the *Washington Post*, he has conducted more than 35,000 past-life regressions and future-life progressions since 1974, helping thousands of patients empower themselves through these techniques. His CDs, cassette tapes and DVDs teach people self-hypnosis, and guide them into past and future lives. He gives lectures and seminars on hypnosis, regression and progression therapy, and conscious dying; he is also a consultant to corporations, attorneys, and the local and network media. His first edition of *The Search for Grace*, was made into a television movie by CBS. His third book, the award winning *Soul Healing*, is a classic on alternative medicine and psychic empowerment. *Past Lives—Future Lives* is Dr. Goldberg's international bestseller and is the first book written on future lives (progression hypnotherapy).

Dr. Goldberg distributes CDs, cassette tapes, and DVDs to teach people self-hypnosis and to guide them into past and future lives and time travel. For information on self-hypnosis tapes, speaking engagements, or private sessions, Dr. Goldberg can be contacted directly by writing to:

Bruce Goldberg, D.D.S., M.S.
4300 Natoma Avenue, Woodland Hills, CA 91364
Telephone: (800) Karma-4-U or (800) 527-6248
Fax: (818) 704-9189
email: drbg@sbcglobal.net
Website: www.drbrucegoldberg.com

Please include a self-addressed, stamped envelope with your letter.

9 781579 681227